The Bride

ESSAYS IN THE CHURCH

By Daniel Berrigan, S.J.

TIME WITHOUT NUMBER
(1957 Lamont Poetry Selection)

THE BRIDE: ESSAYS IN THE CHURCH

The Bride

ESSAYS IN THE CHURCH

Daniel Berrigan, S.J.

New York   THE MACMILLAN COMPANY   1959

Imprimi potest:
    Thomas Henneberry, S.J.

Nihil obstat:
    John A. Goodwine, J.C.D.
    Censor Librorum

Imprimatur:
    ✠ Francis Cardinal Spellman
    Archbishop of New York

December 15, 1958

The nihil obstat and imprimatur are official declarations that a book or pamphlet is free of doctrinal or moral error. No implication is contained therein that those who have granted the nihil obstat and imprimatur agree with the contents, opinions or statements expressed.

First Printing

Library of Congress catalog card number: 59-6980

The Macmillan Company, New York
Brett-Macmillan Ltd., Galt, Ontario

Printed in the United States of America

To Philip

*serious serious My blood says
in its falling*

Contents

Introduction

Regarding the wealth of literature on the meaning of time and history from the Christian standpoint, it would not be too much to say that men of faith have new reason to enter time rationally; not that they have not always been engaged manfully there, but they have been willing for too long to let their activity speak for their beliefs; theories of history adverse to their faith and reason have been allowed to flourish. Especially the material dialectic springing from Hegel and Marx confronts the exciting content of revelation, and demands that a new synthesis be explored.

The problem of faith and history is so many-sided that an indication of different treatments and related problems may not be out of place here. Some scholars have preferred to take up the problem from its sources, and have returned to the Fathers, whose concern with faith and time was in many cases radical. From a study of the Fathers, more than from any other non-inspired source, have come the challenging master ideas whose exploration has so cleared the field of thought today: Incarnation and eschatology, independence of the Church from the cultural and temporal order, theology of the laity, the meaning of the temporal to the Christian, and so on.

Biblical studies have gone ahead under a Papal program remarkable for its liberality: the opportunity is now more than ever at

hand to gather into a pattern the enormous data of scholarship regarding the sacred texts as they refer to the nature of the Church,
and her continuing responsibilities in time.

Again, a new respect is abroad in regard to other religions; it is
a common thing to read sympathetic evaluations of them in relation to the total burden of truth entrusted to the Church. Newman
had put the matter in a good light for future students:

Now the phenomenon, admitted on all hands, is this; that great portions
of what is generally received as Christian truth is in its rudiments or in
its separate parts to be found in heathen philosophies and religions. For
instance, the doctrine of a Trinity is found both in the East and in the
West; so is the ceremony of washing. So is the rite of sacrifice. The
doctrine of the Divine Word is Platonic; the doctrine of the Incarnation
is Indian; of a Divine Kingdom is Judaic; of angels and devils is Magian;
the connection of the body with sin is Gnostic; celibacy is known to
Bonze and Talapoin; a sacerdotal order is Egyptian; the idea of a new
birth is Chinese and Eleusinian; belief in a sacramental system is
Pythagorean; and honors to the dead are polytheism. Such is the nature
of the fact before us.

When many distinctions have been made between the wording
of a doctrine and its content, Newman's passage remains remarkable; it qualifies the older view, which perhaps was slow to recognize
the full implications of the great word Catholic and the Church's
will to respect and assume partial truths, whatever their source.

Missiology, again, is growing into a complicated science that
brings to its aid all resources of learning; cultural, linguistic, historical, anthropological. Here, too, it could be said that thought has
waited for centuries on action; and the first enterprises of the modern
era of the Church were so often disastrous or nearly fruitless owing
to ignorance of method, finality, and degrees of adaptation. But the
missioner can now unite to his zeal a more or less exact knowledge
of what is expected of him precisely qua missioner; where his labors
tend, what are his norms of action, what terms can be made with
local practices. If he is also reinforced by a sense of the finality of
redeemed humanity, the dynamism of the Church in time, it is
clear that his local alarms and setbacks can be put against a more
liberating background.

One could also range far and wide, speculating why the problem of sacred history has come so to the fore in theological thought. On the one hand two wars in a generation have brought an apocalyptic sense to the world; the apparent end of things impresses men with a sense of the end. An exaggerated preparation for a "second coming," a preparation which tends to scorn human values, is the ambiguous fruit of calamity; and is as great a temptation as the bourgeois "settling in" produced by the prosperity of the last century. Civil marriage with the world, or an absolute divorce from it: these are the two faces of the single temptation the present century has offered.

The new frontiers in physical science have forced the issues squarely. Science has speeded time up, and supplied by implication a meaning to its direction; but the term of this synthesis is nothing more than the possession by man of his own world in time. It was perhaps too much to expect of a secularized world that science should seek in revelation the final meaning of its own findings; but it is none the less impossible for theology to ignore the profound breach between itself and the new world which science has opened up. The task of theology is, as always, to insist upon the eternal destiny of man; to show the Church's compatibility with the life and action of the new world; to assert again a respect for the human uses of matter and the way in which human effort can be gathered into the Divine synthesis made known in Christ and continued in His Church.

A scientific world has succeeded the one in which theology illumined man's conduct and gave it a direction; the new science has shown the pliability of time under its hand; it has crowded time with new discovery and sense experience, while offering neither direction nor meaning outside its own phenomenology; but in spite of radical limitation science holds out the hope of a secular unity and peace. One world, but no other world. Peace, but within the enslavement of time, and with its vicissitudes and cycles still unbroken.

What is the function of time according to the new science? Time is the instrument supreme for the human act; since eternity is simply not a datum, time must function to bring about those hopes formerly placed beyond it. Human values, established and built up in time, are everything; what is of real value is whatever builds the secular city; profoundly "sensible," pragmatic, and monolithic.

The UN building on New York's East Side is a symbol of the synthetic urge of the world, an urge which confronts the Mystical Body with a modern secular counterpart. A counterpart, not a counterfeit; unless men like Pius XII, Suhard, Saliège, and a host of others are to be ignored; but an expression of the deepest longings of men in this age; and according to an eminent Catholic anthropologist, Teilhard de Chardin, an expression of the term of the Divine will is an evolving universe; from non-life to life, from simplicity of life to an organism, from the single organism to a primitive community, thence to a consciousness of the common life of nations; the advance of man, with ever greater liberty and intelligence, toward the true unity of humanity itself. "It is not superman who is to be born in this higher plane of evolution; it is humanity."

The great need stands clear. If a crude barbarism is not to be succeeded by a civilized one, if superman is not to be born instead of the community of the world, the Divine thought with respect to man's conquest of time and matter must continue to be elucidated; and that Divine thought would seem to demand, with the passing of time, that matter be progressively informed by the action of the Holy Spirit, that blind instinct yield to reasonable action illumined by grace, that independence of time replace enslavement to it.

In the beginning, God created heaven and earth. But in the course of history, the Savior has disrupted human history with the accessible gifts of grace, the Spirit has been promised and has come, remaining in the world to act upon souls. In the fulness of time, at an hour known only to the Father, the Son returns as judge. This is in barest outline the mysterious plan of sacred history.

History as a science has motion, measurable or measured, as its material object, and human freedom for a *sine qua non*. So history is not merely a series of acts placed in time; the mark of history is always the repeated free act in time. History then begins with time, and time with creation. The first act of history was creation, which also marked the commencement of time itself. This was the remarkable analysis of St. Augustine.

But the nature of history, considered absolutely, cannot be lim-

ited to a physics or a philosophy; the knowledge of creation is a
datum of a supernatural revelation; we are immediately, if we seek
the highest meaning of history, on a theological plane. And not only
the fact of creation is revealed; but man is created with a supernatural destiny from the beginning; God has revealed Himself as
acting *ad extra*; an eternal order, involving rational beings, is being
unfolded in time. So a sacred history is in no sense a "construct,"
such as, for example, a philosophy of history would be. It is not
difficult to conclude with Dawson that only a Christian can enter
sympathetically into the idea of a sacred history; it is faith which
opens the door here. Père Henry has pointed out the astonishing
unaninimity of philosophers and theologians with regard to the fact
that the Judaic-Christian view alone is capable of giving a meaning
to history:

Independently of the fact of Christianity, there is no history in the
objective sense, that is to say, there is no direction in the unfolding of
events or of historical structures. Independently of Christian thought,
even though it may be at times distorted or actually denied, there is no
historical knowledge which can be raised to the level of a philosophy of
history, or in which can be found the meaning of history. This is certainly
an imposing and astonishing affirmation. It is a statement which should
be tempered and made more precise, but I state it bluntly because—
whether it be right or wrong—it is the unanimous conclusion of the
authors whose names I have just mentioned (e.g., Marrou, Aron,
Guitton, Fessard, Monchanin, Barth, Brunner, Cullmann, Bouyer,
Aubert, Daniélou, Malevez, Haecker, etc.).

And this because in almost every other civilization one or another of the requirements of a true history is lacking; the nature of
time is misunderstood, or human freedom is denied. Time is regarded variously as a mirage, a reflection or mode of eternity, a series
of meaningless and ineluctable cycles; renewal and incarnation proceeding endlessly, or a bare and vicious plane of existence which
must be escaped at all cost—into nirvana or a world of ideal forms,
if the seeker after God is ever to reach Him.

Human freedom is also gravely misunderstood outside the
Hebraic-Christian tradition. In the Greek scheme, the law so im-
poses itself on man as to bind him to itself with an eternal necessity.

Subjection to the law is the only final law; the virtuous man puts himself to the wheel with a minimum of concern, and endures. The others resist and are destroyed. It makes no difference whether their sin was blind, or unforeseen, or not a matter of their deepest consciousness at all; the transgressor must pay. It is easy to see how a purely material concept enveloping moral evil induced a mood of pessimism which permeates Greek tragedy; how such a concept robbed Greek historians of their richest source of inspiration, and reduced them to a series of spectators of life.

They were robbed from another direction too. History was for them the necessary act repeated; its meaning was not within itself at all; the historian's work was a matter of imposition from without, a construction. The data of history were one or another of the eternal cycles. The historian could tell of the going forth or the return, of wars and peace, of the life of the city and country; but in all these it was the cycle that guided him; that cycle which was mirrored somewhat in the nights and days, the seasons and years, but which was in fact more ironbound and undeflecting than they.

Let the historian narrate the event and follow the wheel; but an inquiry after meanings was not for him. More: it never should occur to him to look for a history in any meaningful or human sense at all.

Whose task was it? It belonged to the poet, Vates, maker and seer. He it was who could take scissors in hand and cut the cycle; he could determine, in a sublime *jeu d'esprit*, that such and such an event had beginning and end. He of all men could untangle the raveled skein of cause and effect that wound all men into its inescapable circle.

So the quasi-religious nature of the poet; he gave a rationale to the dealings of the gods; he justified to men the ways of the Divine, and so rendered them more tolerable. He imposed a beginning and an end on continuity: not only these—but he gave a relief to the dead stretch of destiny, by elevating his material at a certain point where the tangle begins to spring free; he gave the cycle a "middle," a discontinuity, a point where the rational seeking sense could view the beginning in the end. So the poet was theologian, historian, and prophet in one: his performances were the rite par excellence; he stood honorably superior to annalist and priest, for he alone could be said truly to "enter" the event and give it a meaning—not so much by metaphysical dissection as by main force of creation; he made events into something.

It was to the poet, then, that Greek culture looked for guidance in the search for meaning in history; he made the transfer from cycle, law, necessity, to a true and free history. The poetic function was so elaborated by Aristotle, whose scant respect is evident for the historian, left on the sideline of reality with not much more than a chart of dates for his achievement.

So in the ancient pagan atmosphere of flux, escape, and renewal, the concept of a true history was swallowed up in a mist of nature-theology, ignorant of the meaning of time and human freedom, seeking release and significance in the portrayal of certain ideal figures. The men in the myth were to represent the passion, aspiration, continuity, interference, defeat, and nobility which mark the Divine-human relationship. Under the poet's hand the immutable cycle was relieved by assertion of independence along the way, by prayers momentarily answered, by escape from physical and moral danger, by warnings, alarms, and reprisals—by all those noble postponements of the inevitable which classical tragedy includes. The theater was the temple; sacred history as an artistic universe existed between the entrance and resolution of the action; and though according to classical formula the law stood at the end vindicated and unstained by human contact, for a few hours an impossibly wonderful effort had been made to burst the cyclic chain; and the exhaustion of player and witness was not altogether unrelieved by joy and relief; joy in the liberation from fear, relief in a very human pity for the hero—a pity which inserted humanism into the iron march of event. So while tragedy remained a noble example of humanism, it was also an act of religion.

Still, pessimism was unlit from within. Hope was a god on wheels, pushed out from the wings of time.

And even if a deity entered history to light it with his sacred presence, he was immediately swallowed in the cycle he thought to rupture; the event which dreamed of being unique, of working a change, was itself forced into the pattern; the theology of incarnation became part of the tradition; the god himself was planted, flowered, died with the seasons. The hero, the god, and the ideal world of both were governed by the law from which neither could long escape. Or else it happened that the pantheon stretched upward into an infinite number and division; or if the supreme god was reached, he was found also bound to earth, to renewal, to human vice and strife. Never nirvana. The law had won, interminably, and the lawgiver had never shown his face.

I

Israel

God, Who in divers tongues . . . spoke through the prophets . . . in the fulness of time spoke through His Son.

The paradoxes of sacred history as it unfolded in Israel are intolerable to the unbeliever. The chosen people are a social nonentity on the historical scene. Abraham is singled out, inexplicably, from a nomad tribe, transported by a revelation to a place apart, and given a covenant which immediately expands his hope into the promise of a nation numerous as the stars of the heavens, as the sands of the shore. It is this summons to an obscure herdsman which opens the direction of sacred history. Biblical history begins in a line rather than in a circle: a God absolutely independent of nature, transcending all cycles, a Law Which is a Person; the end is predicted darkly from the very beginning, but the end is totally other than the beginning, and the course of progress can never turn upon itself. Implied already is a free response in time to a Divine call, a decision to observe and follow, an entrance of the Divine in human affairs. Later, at the Incarnation, the continuity of the Plan is to be exploded without being destroyed; its course will continue undeflected at a deeper stratum of religious experience, grace, and suffering.

But from Abraham to Bethlehem, time will be utilized and

valued to the utmost by friend and by enemy of God. The holy impatience of the prophets, who see and reveal progressively the central hour and the Person Who comes; the national lists of kings with their moral gloss on character and work; exile and return; apostasy and penance; these are only the various and magnificent deviations on the straight line—the clear path through time, from the first hour to the hour when God speaks through His Son.

So the paradox of sacred history deepens frequently into tragedy, because choice involves rejection; and the pages of the Bible are heavy with the shards of rejected nations. Babylon is excluded, though she is consumed with a cosmic restlessness, her triremes reaching the farthest known shores; or again, nations are overlooked who have left a luminous trail through the centuries; original and noble art forms, a genius for government or conquest; so that if one were seeking in Israel for natural basis for the action of grace, a basis in taste or wisdom or genius— But none of these is involved: My election is in Juda.

Indeed, the mediocrity of the Hebrew people extends in almost every direction, except of course in that vast vertical direction which points to the regard of God—the eternal predeliction for His sons. On the map of the world Israel is little more than a corner; her archaeology reveals a meager and utilitarian mode of life; she has little taste for speculation; the tragic form of drama is unknown to her; no epic poet enshrines her national history in a frame that would make her a type and model of emergent peoples. She lives, for all but one thing, completely submerged in the sea of history. It is only the Divine choice that has given her survival; a choice enshrined in a series of books written under His order and collaboration.

But the paradox of Israel extends even into her own identity and her knowledge of it. In the fullness of time, in that moment when the deepest meaning is to give to her Divine history, when her millennium is to bear its transcendent Flower, and she will witness in a Jewish Face all her own fulfillment—in that hour Israel turns from her God, incarnate in an individual Jewish nature. She does not know Him. His Features are other than those that pride and envy have imposed on her imagination. They are the Features of suffering Job, Isaiah, the Psalmists; but a tradition born of fiercest self-interest had never allowed those Features to appear as archetypical, as founding a true hope of what was to come to her. Would the Messiah answer the national longing? He would burst the national wall and allow the world to stream into the sanctuary. Would He bring wealth and honor once more to Israel, ruling from a throne surrounded by spiritual satraps? He would rule from a tree. The supreme overthrowal of that hour is summed up by the Jew Paul: "We preach Christ crucified . . . to the Jews a scandal."

How describe the disruption of that nation which had been the fulcrum of God's action on the world, in that hour when the Lord came to her? Her world was overturned, her seams shaken out, her utter poverty revealed. "The diminution of these is the fulness of the Gentiles." Poured out on the earth, the seed of Jewish truth that had starved on Jewish stones grew into that tree to which the nations of the four winds flock.

That point of sacred history which should have been her eternal triumph witnessed her fall. Jerusalem, a city of peace, symbol of national unity for centuries, so beautiful as to be a figure for heaven itself; Jerusalem could have been the heart of the world, the city whose towers only the apocalypse would shake. In her history her sins had resulted in temporary estrangements from God; now her fate is all but settled; the effects of this sin will follow her through all time.

Sacred history, then, enters a new phase with the Incarnation and the establishment of the Church. Heretofore that history had been a matter of written revelation, under various literary forms. Israel's sin had been the willful illusion that she could ignore the content of her own sacred books, and still retain her national identity. But while the Divine Spirit was always at the elbow of His amanuensis, and on the tongues of her prophets, there was no guarantee that her people would learn and accept the lesson of God. And her eventual misreading of her own texts was so grievous that at the fullness of her history she stood a stranger to herself; a gate for the nations instead of their inner sanctuary, a signpost for the generations, destined to remain far from her own home. The opposition that confronted the Savior so implacably is a vivid lesson in her self-betrayal—the struggle with which her myth won over her revelation;

the twelve judges of the nations, the secular parousia, Israel again dominant over her Roman oppressor, her despising of the gentiles in her midst, her attempts to make of David's King a little local magistrate whose powers were turned wholly toward self-interest; her erection of the law into an absolute, supplanting the Lawgiver.

She had tried to curve the linear course of her history—a course mysteriously traced by her prophets—into a closed circle no less impenetrable than that of the imperial pagan nations. She sought the establishment of Israel as a theocratic power in this world, the return of her displaced peoples, the building of the symbolic wall that would make Jerusalem, in a radical sense, the closed city. What she really sought, in effect, was a speedy conclusion to the Divine event; a shortening of that road which was meant to stretch outward in time, transforming her from a provincial tribe into a nation that would enlighten the world. Her deliberate choice was the corruption of that promise she had guarded so well from without, only to have it destroyed at home. It was a way of "escape"; a determination to telescope the time, so that her parousia would be joined by force to her vindication before the world.

From the moment of her self-betrayal, Israel ceases to be the center of sacred history. She is elbowed to the fringe of events; her unity is scattered, her religious sense vitiated; she is no longer the unique object of Divine love, the unique deposit of truth. God will cease to speak through her prophets, to find her sacrifice pleasing, to surround her wanderings with His presence. Her very existence in time will henceforth be shrouded in mystery, the end of which is known dimly by the newly chosen nations, but ignored by herself; an end involving her humiliation before the Son of her own son David; an end postponed for centuries until the Son of David will again turn upon her a human face, because she has turned to Him in faith at last. Her theology is frozen in a form meant to have been transitional toward closer union, greater glory. Though her sacred eminence remains undeniable, since she bore the Savior into the world, so does her shame; deliberately, and as a matter of religious policy, she chose not to know Him. She has become now like the nations who tried her history so sorely—an instrument of Divine anger, a lesson in the effects of apostasy. Her temple is destroyed;

and its destruction is the signal for the nations of the earth to go in and possess her riches.

So the continuity of the Divine plan was disrupted without being in any sense destroyed. The tortuous path of Jewish history expanded into a Roman highway, but the point of juncture is always clear. The period of pedagogy was summed up in an hour; the time of manifestation was begun. Sacred history entered a new phase, more nobly synthesized, marked by unique hours; now the *gesta Dei* which broke up for the Jew the inhuman cycles of the pagan world are themselves excelled by the single Fact, the God born of woman. Pagan pessimism is again and finally answered: sin and unbelief only succeed in sending sacred history into deeper and more painful channels, into a richer harvest.

II

The Event

The event par excellence has occurred. In this statement will be summed up all the past and all the future course of sacred history. It will determine the root difference between the nature of Israel and the Church; the accessibility of grace, the action of the Holy Spirit in time, the power of the living Exemplar, the attitude of Christians toward the world of cultures, of scientific progress, toward the world at large and toward one another.

The first stage accomplished in Israel was one of preparation. There was no "center" in which the Old Testament Jew could rest definitively through his history, as though all were accomplished; all his destiny and meaning were in his hope. The Divine interventions in prophecy, miracle, material aid, had one end only—to reinforce and purify that hope, to remind the nation that she was waiting, that she had not yet arrived, was not yet at rest, not yet herself. Punishment purified her heart in order to give her access to that God Who would grant her His Son. Her great men were types of her greatest Man. The bronze serpent that cured her ills in the desert prefigured the Lord healing from the cross; the manna that fell to feed her symbolized the Bread of Life. The passage of the Red Sea traced the spiritual journey of the soul, out of the bondage of sin, into baptism and the freedom of God's sons. Israel takes up manfully the task of her own spiritualization by unending sacrifice and prayer; but all her rites await supplanting and perfecting by the action of Another. She is perpetual Advent. Her books give a profoundly moving vision of a nation conscious of imperfection, labor, hope; her whole weight and center of gravity is placed in a Future; the future, indeed, is the common tense of her national voice—"He shall come . . . He shall reign. . . . When the hour is come . . . The Desired of the nations . . . Come, oh come!"

But with the Incarnation, the phase of announcement, of preparation, is over. The Mystery, in St. Paul's great word, is present, is incarnate in time. Formerly, when the tide of sacred history had cast aside from its mainstream nations outside Israel and even individuals within her, Israel stood firm; now she is to be put to the test, and in her greatest hour, to be found wanting.

But for the nations, hope is swallowed in fulfillment; the future loses its agony in a present filled with glory; preparation yields to welcome. "The Word was made Flesh, and dwelt among us." Still, the ideas of hope and preparation do not entirely disappear from history; they only face a different term; the end of things. The Master, in appearing, fulfills in His sacred Person the weight of faith and hope living in Israel; but He represents another hope, and casts it forward, into another future: His second coming. And this is true, even though the great Fact has already been accomplished in Christ; the faith and hope of Israel have flowered in the Church of the nations.

Again, up to the Incarnation, the sacred books of Juda were the instrument of continuity for sacred history. Now the Church enters the scene to preserve, amplify, and interpret the same history. Her act of preservation looks to the past; she is the Divinely appointed guardian of the message given Israel and misread by her blindness. In this sense the Church guards her own history; she guarantees the continuity of the familial line which has borne her as fruit. She finds in the Old Testament the partial credentials for her claims; but her truest credentials are her authority as interpreter of the sacred books; to give, against the weight of national jealousies, against the paganism and pride of the centuries, a witness to the Divine intention in first entrusting His word to men. And by preserving Israel's

trust, she is also constituted judge over Israel; she is the instrument
of God with respect to the rejected nation; it is she who will stand
and endure through time, so that the perverse nation may find in
her the features of Israel's own Son on the day of the great return.

The Church also amplifies sacred history, in a physical and
mystical sense. The Mystery was in Israel in a closed vessel of election;
the new Israel has broken the vessel and opened its treasures to
nourish the earth. But her amplification also extends vertically into
man's nature; because Christ lives in His Church through time, she
has the Spirit of Christ, the example of Christ, and the Body of
Christ to transform the souls she is sent to. Her amplitude in history
is her self-release in every soul, in every civilization and nation, freed
from the taint of pride and secularism which destroyed Israel. She
takes literally the order of the Master, "Going, preach the Gospel
to every creature. . . ."

In amplifying the horizon of her effort, the Church makes her
own the culture of every period; she has no color to her Body, no
distinctive habits or custom set up in opposition, or as characteristic
of her. She speaks every language, and her welcome to men is in
their own accent, leading to a true home:

A priest at the altar has no face, and the arms that raise
the Lord are without dust or ornament . . .
Your servants wear garments that do not grow old, and your speech
is like the metal of your bells . . .
For the measure of your faith is not as the faith of man, and
the measure of your years knows no autumn. . . .
It is you who pray over all tombs! . . .
You are the only sign of the eternal on this earth; all that
you do not transmute is transmuted by death.

But it is in her living interpretation of the books of the Old
and New Testaments that her most striking contrast with Israel lies.
In this self-awareness, this consciousness of who she is, lies the
Church's disruption of the Israelitic stream of history. She looks to
the books of Juda only as a secondary proof for her claims. If she
seeks justification before the nations of man, it is not chiefly to legal
documents of the promise that she points, but to the will of the God

Who wrote them. In this sense she completes, synthesizes, clarifies the inspired word; she is herself an immensely more powerful proof of her claim than are the sacred books. She herself is the new covenant, not primarily entrusted to writing, but expressed expansively in her own life, her development through time, her interpretation of the truth entrusted to her, the growth of the Divine seed cast into her womb. From henceforth her task will lie in the sharing of the fruits of her self-contemplation. To ensure the continuity of the task, Christ establishes a hierarchic Body to which He grants absolute custody of the Sacred deposit, not totally contained in writings, but in the Body which owns them.

Perhaps "interpret" is therefore a feeble term; the function of the Church, with respect to the Bible, is one of absolute ownership by the Body of Christ; implying all the rights of a living voice and mind over the historical letter, the book once written.

So the data of sacred history are transferred from the page to the actions of a living Body. The historian, armed with faith, no longer looks to the Bible alone for his criterion as to progress, setbacks, development. His chief study must fall on the free actions of the Mystical Body; primarily on the teaching Church, then on the believing response of the faithful as on an accurate reflection. And he knows that the Body has not finished its action in time; its documents only express the riches of its self-consciousness to this or that hour, clarifying the destiny it has so far achieved; but it will have more to say of itself and its relation to the world. In continually reading its own past and achieving its present, the living exegesis of time goes on.

So it is the Body of Christ, the Church, with which the student of sacred history must deal. This statement marks a change extending even to the historian himself. He is transformed by faith (without which he has no access to the mystery) from a believing outsider, reading a historical text, to a believing member, himself involved in, sharing, and in a sense helping to make her history. There are no pure spectators at this drama, if its true course is to be traced at all. From within the Body, sharing its Divine life and action, the sacred historian shares in the growth of the Body, even while he interprets it, since he is himself penetrated by its Spirit, and weighted by its destiny.

As the Church continues in time, she is to become progressively the leaven of the world. This immediately places her in a situation which Israel never had to face. Israel was to remain a closed system. As a matter of the Divine will, the purity of her message was to be protected at all costs; and the cost was a "no trespassing" sign fronting the nations; her attitude to the world was one of armed neutrality. God made known His absolute will in this regard, in a hundred ways, and punished its transgression terribly. Conquered pagan cities were often leveled; to protect against intermarriage and contamination the conquered peoples were put to the sword. Introduction of foreign gods or rites was the capital sin, punished as no other. When Israel was in material need, she was to look to Him only. In periods of captivity it may have been temporarily impossible to obey in all rigor the command forbidding her to deal with the heathen, so she assimilated details of culture, modes of work, language, even certain foreign elements into the sacred writings. But in all that touched her vocation and task in history: the knowledge of God's nature, the structure of her worship—her independence must remain absolute.

To her enforced isolation then, Israel owed the purity and continuity of her religious message. Her sacred history was a thing apart from the course of world history; the two were separate and sealed compartments. Interpenetration or leavening of the world were sternly forbidden her; one of the marks of Israel was precisely her noncatholicity.

As a result, there is no real problem of secular history in relation to Israel. She was not in world history, in any significant way at all—as, say, Babylon or Egypt is in it. Nor did she allow world history to exist in her, except for those times of exile or captivity when she was swallowed up in the great world systems, and entered their ledgers as a minor conquest, a jealous, exclusive, and suspicious segment of empire which preferred death to assimilation. But for those periods of history when Israel followed the Divine destiny without serious deviation, without undue presssure from her enemies or schism among her own, when her knowledge of her identity was strongest, at those periods her whole instinct was one of apartness, of indifference to world history. She was her own history, a sacred one incomprehensible to the unbeliever, a deliberate and closely guarded mystery.

And as she refused to enter the world, she just as jealously refused to be penetrated by it. Even in her national humiliation, an elaborate legal system of clean and unclean, of rite, blessing, and purification, protected the environs of her altars and kept her sacrifice unsullied. Was there ever in history such a "different" national entity, keeping to its own path for so many centuries? God called her again and again a "stiff-necked people." Her neighbors perhaps had equal reason to complain. Unalterably conservative, opposed unto death to change, to adjustment, to coming to terms, to being included—these were her marks.

The shifting forms of her national life were also determined in great part by the same consideration: the exigencies of her theology. When preservation demanded a nomadic life, she took to any roads, or built them as she went; when the Revelation told her to possess a land, then and only then she settled down. She left on history no indication that she ever developed the plastic arts; because the nations surrounding her had sacrilegiously carved and adored the works of their hands, her theophanies had forbidden these as an abomination. But she left a marvelous body of literature that she might perpetuate in poetry, law, history, and prophecy the pure deposit of her ancestors' faith. Her whole character and élan, finally, were determined by one necessity: the preservation of what was granted to her alone on earth; her exclusive privilege to prepare for, and to bear into time, the Savior.

These reflections will help to open the question of the Church and history, of her catholicity and the terms on which she must meet her world. Unlike Israel, the Church has been denied the protective exclusiveness of the old covenant; her attitude, as she faces the world at any given time, is centrifugal. Christ has established her as the light of the world; her good works are to shine before men; her gospel is to be preached to every creature.

This central problem of sacred history, the relation of the Church to the world in time, has nowhere been examined with more profundity and understanding than in the work of P. Daniélou. A few quotations will open his line of thought:

"Christianity is in history. . . . Profane history enters into sacred history. . . . But these forms of Christianity will always be corruptible and transitory. It is necessary for the Church, once it has put them on, to throw them off again, as old garments." The time between the Incarnation and the second coming is "one of waiting. . . . It is the time in which we are living." The Christian no longer "awaits victory; he awaits the enjoyment of those goods which have been already acquired for him, and which he does not yet possess. . . ."

Now during this time of waiting, this delay between victory and acquisition, what of the old world, the world of secular history? "Henceforth it is departed; the heavenly Jerusalem with its new heavens and its new earth, the world of the Transfiguration, is already present, but it is not yet made manifest. Meantime the old world receives a sort of reprieve for the role it must still play." . . . "The mystery of the present time is that it actually contains this simultaneous presence of a past world which lingers on in it, and of a future world already existing in an anticipated fashion." But what makes the world of secular history "past"?—its being "radically surpassed by the world of the Church, which is the future already present."

The world, then, as P. Daniélou views it, is "past" because it is surpassed by the excellence of the Church, already present within it. But if one were to follow this line of argument logically, would he not be forced to conclude that the Church herself, considered purely as an external "organization" in time, is a thing of reprieve, is anachronistic, with respect to the world of grace already operating invisibly in and through her? Such a comparison, between objects of different orders, has a certain amount of validity; but it can never be a substitute for an analysis of each of the terms within its own sphere. For if Father Daniélou's comparison reveals the superior nature of one term (the Church), it still tells very little of the nature of excellence of the other ("temporal society," "this world," "the temporal city").

Does "this world" of secular history become a thing of reprieve, "an anachronism," in comparison with the superior excellence of the leaven which works on it? One can only speak here, with Gustave Thils, of a confusion of values, the reproving and dismissal of an object for not being what it was never meant to be:

Fr. Daniélou uses the following example to illustrate his position: The temporal order, even after the appearance of Christianity, maintains its *raison d'être* for a time. Adopting, in a new sense, the image of St. Irenaeus, we can say that the entirety of profane history is the shoot of the vine on which grows the grape of the Church. When the grape appears, the shoot has only to be cast aside. But between the wintertime of the shoot and the summertime of the grape, there is the spring in which the grape, still flowering, has need of the shoot to support it, awaiting the day when the Church shall have attained her maturity, and the world can pass away, having fulfilled its purpose.

This example, as Daniélou indicates, is borrowed out of context; Irenaeus is referring to the Jewish nation which was cast aside when the fullness of time came. But even within the discussion it is necessary to point out that there was no necessity of Israel's being cast aside; she need only have been fulfilled and assimilated. Her rejection was not a matter of the logical development of her own destiny; it was consequent upon her bad will and blindness.

Now to suppose that temporal society represents an analogous case is perhaps to prejudge the world where no source of revelation has done so. More, such an attitude seems to ignore the positive human values of time toward building up the Body of Christ in its temporal aspect; values of culture, civilization, technical progress without whose assimilation the Church would remain a society apart; a society which would reveal, with respect to the full life of man, a tendency to poverty and reaction.

The question here is one of stress between the two poles of Incarnation in the world of time, and the arrival of the "world of the transfiguration." Daniélou's conclusion is nothing less than admirable, "But its role (that is, human progress) is to lead humanity to a more perfect maturity in order to furnish grace with a richer subject. In this sense, work for the progress of humanity enters into the Plan of Providence and hastens the growth of the Church which needs, in order to attain its plenitude, the sap of the vine which bears it. This defines the position of the Church in relation to the temporal order. It will not be one of depreciation, because this order plays a role in the Plan of Providence. But the Christian will avoid exalting it, since its role remains entirely subordinate."

Daniélou's preoccupation is with "fulfillment"; he is concerned with the "ambiguity" of human progress, with its possibility of turning to the bad as well as to the good, "depending on whether the means of power which it offers humanity through science and organization are used in one way or another." He will concede only this value to profane history, that it "gives to the Church the material she transfigures by grace."

This is all well and good; but there is a strong case also for a more positive defense of the secular world in time, for pleading its adaptability to the action of grace. "Human progress is ambiguous"; but it is still governed mysteriously by Providence; the issue is not equally set between good and evil as between two positive entities of equal strength. *Gratia perficit naturam* reveals the essence of the natural itself, which is patient of a supernatural invasion; if profane history gives the Church the material she transfigures by grace, it remains true that an obedient "transfigurability" is of the essence of nature; that evil comes to it from outside its nature, not from the material or formal constitutives; that evil comes from what Father Daniélou and we would agree on calling "use."

Again the potential of the temporal order has already been demonstrated by the way the Divine Action has fallen on it, at its supreme hour, by supplying a human Body for the Son of God. Now, if one speaks of the end of the natural world as simply "casting aside," he must take exception to the revealed fact; the human nature assumed by the Word was assumed once forever; It shares the eternal glory of the Trinity, and welcomes the risen bodies of the just into its company. These bodies, including the Savior's, are surely part of that material order which one might, apart from revelation, see as merely passing away; more, as "cast aside."

St. Paul, however, saw creation groaning for the new birth, all irrational nature joining in the longings of men for liberation, a birth which is simultaneous with the second coming. One recalls the liturgy, which speaks in relation to the dead, *vita mutatur, non tollitur.* It is certain that some part of the material world is so excellent that it will share eternity; that it already possesses, by its union with the soul, the "seed of glory."

Now, it would seem to be a healthy principle that any order of things is to be judged by the most excellent parts that constitute it; so one would arrive at a true judgment of the world in time, not by being preoccupied with its purely non-viable, corruptible elements, but with the part upon which the Divine Action has rested in an altogether transcendent way. Then: if some material elements are capable of assumption by the Divine, can the material world be evaluated properly in the scheme of sacred history by placing its term as a mere "passing away"?

One would prefer to speak of assimilation and fulfillment. The Mystical Body of Christ operates in time; its seigneury is an absolute one, over the total creation; over all civilizations, all tongues, all technocracy and learning, all art and science. It is true to say that these things "give to the Church the material which she transfigures"; but is it the whole truth? She transfigures them by assuming them to herself. Their mode of existence at the last day is not taken away; it is only changed. Any restriction placed on the Church from entrance into the values of its material world only transfers a kind of Docetism from the physical Body of Christ to His Mystical Body.

Again, is it stating the whole case to speak of the world as "material" for the transforming action of the Church? It is mere material only in the same sense that "slime of the earth" in Genesis is the literal material for the creation of the body of man. In both cases we are speaking of the "secondary matter" of the schoolmen, material already highly organized and complex. In the case at hand, that of the present material world, we are confronted with a hierarchic world of being, containing not an absolute minimum of beauty and truth, but an expanding maximum; a natural image of God which through history has always nourished the theologian and the mystic with its profundity and mystery: and which continues to reveal God in its progressive humanization.

III

Beginnings

The notion of perdurance in time is a very attractive and powerful one for the mind. Man is delighted by contemplation of the Winged Victory of Samothrace; not only by its compelling grandeur, but by considering the thousands of years in which it has signaled and elevated the presence of the beautiful, for men long dead. It is the same with ancient poetry; the same with the ideal of democracy, with the life of religion. These things have known a life on earth which refuses to die; which may be suppressed or ignored for one or another unfortunate period, but which returns to claim the heart, to influence decisions and new creations.

In speaking of the longevity of the Church, one should begin by pointing out that there are various objects, ideas, institutions, racial groups whose life on the earth is much more extended than hers. The quality of apostolicity does not attempt to claim the longest actual perdurance in time for the Church; such a claim would have had no meaning at all for her first years, when she was a newcomer, a phenomenon of a few days or a few years. And even if she is regarded today, other objects and institutions much older than herself confront her; old works of art, old alphabets, historical traces of primitive man, and so on.

But the mere fact of lastingness in time is, of course, not the point at issue; the apostolicity of the Church, like her unity, her holiness, her catholicity, is an absolutely unique and intrinsic mark of her being, something that belongs to her alone, something that was hers from the beginning, and could never be claimed by any other structure. It is not enough to say merely that the Church is apostolic because she has withstood time. She has also endured as herself; she has always taught the same truth, exercised the same means toward holiness, preserved the Papacy. Surely, the fact that an institution should preserve its identity for many centuries, adhering to the form and ideal that first created it, is a marvelous indication of internal vitality. But again, such a quality is theoretically possible to a body other than the Church. There is, for example, a religious minority among the Jews, small and almost unheard, that still worships according to the instructions of Deuteronomy or Leviticus, believes what Abraham believed, prays as he prayed, awaits what he awaited. The fact remains that such a religious attitude is in error today; that the law has been canceled by the fact of the Incarnation now some thousands of years old. But the full idea of Catholic apostolicity is not explained merely by saying that the Church has endured for some twenty centuries, or even by saying that she is still herself, that she has preserved a certain body of truth.

For the Church is a mystery. She continues the Incarnation in time. And as the extension of the Word Incarnate, doing what He came to do in His mortal flesh, she shares in the mystery that surrounds His coming. The qualities which set her apart, if they are to reveal her interior features, will be bathed at the same time in a darkness that will keep men forever at a certain distance from her. One does not, for example, reach the depths of that mystery of Christ which St. Paul says is "the very fulness of the Father" by explaining the negative possibility of the Incarnation of a God Whose existence one had reached through speculation alone. So with the Church; to penetrate His Mystical Body one must take one's stand within the body, by faith: "No one comes to me except the Father draw him. . . ." Otherwise the approach to mystery remains speculative, exterior, a kind of intellectual autopsy: "It is only the spirit of Christ which gives life. . . ." and the spirit of Christ is a gift to those whom the Father has called to faith in His Son, faith in His Church.

To come, then, to the apostolic character of the Church, faith claims for her perdurance in time and perdurance in time as herself—but the whole magnificent quality is given her as something unique, a mystery, a grace promised and conferred on her by God Himself. Her apostolicity is a quality of her life, secret and interior, founded on no human ingenuity or vitality, but flowing directly from the eternal Trinity; an immutability of essence, a life which expands, adapts, grows, assimilates, reproduces. But her life at the same time defeats and surpasses all natural analogy by the breadth of opposites which it is able to include. So the Church is at once immortal and in time; her life circulates in the whole Body and in each of the justified, a gift residing in fragile vessels, a life which promises and grants eternity here and now, a life which has the power of placing those on earth in communion with those who share the vision of the Father; a life which has not violated, denied, or suppressed time, but which has simply used it as an instrument of achieving eternity.

The Church, then, did not wait upon the passage of centuries in order to become apostolic, any more than she needed a certain amount of time in order to become catholic or one or holy. What she has she had from the beginning; what she is she was at her birth. All that time has done for her is to manifest openly the qualities conferred on her by the Savior; but just as her exigency, in the tiny upper room of Pentecost, already carried her in desire, in mandate, in destiny, to the ends of the earth, so, at Calvary, at Pentecost, she already knew who she was. She had been given a name; she could no more alter her nature with the passage of time than Christ our Lord in the years of His life could renounce His Divine nature; when she issued from the side of the Savior she had already attained the fullness of Christ, of which St. Paul speaks. In the death of the Savior is her birth, and the conferring of her name, as was promised in Isaias: "I have called thee by thy name; thou art mine." She was given the name which St. Paul would later reveal in the Holy Spirit: "You are the Body of Christ . . . you are one Body, with a single Spirit." And this name was already a Divine thing, creative, instantaneous, effecting what it said. It did not correspond to a quality that would gradually reach her self-consciousness. When the moment of naming the Church came, the Church was created, the Church knew herself, she repeated her name by the Holy Spirit; a name that was immutable, apostolic, having an unbreakable link with the Trinity in truth and holiness. So when her first men came from the upper room after the Spirit had descended on her, the Church was already, in a plenary way, self-conscious. She was able to do in the fullest sense what the man of reason can do in regard to his own existence: to affirm self-identity in a judgment. But the Church, by the power of God, can go far beyond the certitude of reason in declaring her unchanging nature, in revealing progressively, by a law of her inner life, the riches of her self-knowledge. She could say at the moment of her creation: "I know who I am; I will always be what I am; I am the vessel of truth now, at this moment of my birth; I will always have the total truth, because of the Holy Spirit Who is my soul, because of the Word Incarnate Who is my head, because of the Father Whose life I share. I am the secret of the Trinity; I stand revealed, visible, the very fullness of God."

The Holy Spirit will later reveal her formula in Paul; but it is here from the beginning: "(This secret of Christ's) was never made known to any human being in past ages, as it has now been revealed by the Spirit to his holy apostles and prophets, and it is this; that through the Gospel preaching the Gentiles are to win the same inheritance, to be made part of the same body, to share the same Divine promise, in Christ Jesus . . . making known to the Gentiles the unfathomable riches of Christ . . . publishing to the world the plan of this mystery, kept hidden from the beginning of time in the all-creating mind of God. Made manifest now in the Church (is) the subtlety of God's wisdom" (Ephesians).

So in considering the Church's apostolicity, one is considering her as she was, as she is, as she will always be. This is not to deny that in time she also is subject to succession; that being the militant Body of Christ she has a past, a present, a future; it is only to admit by faith that her essence is not subject to the change which succession brings to all but herself. She is the thought of God, and therefore unique, total, all-inclusive. She is the bride of God, to whom He has whispered, once for all, the secret of His name. Possessing the Spirit of the Father as her soul, that Spirit Who is the substantial love of the Father for the Son, her interior features are those of the

Holy Spirit, and she turns toward the Father, forever recognized, forever approved and beloved.

When the believer considers her apostolicity today, then, he does so as a member of the Body; and he declares, through her: "I too am apostolic; I too have an indestructible link with the first moment of the Church's creation. I am present ontologically at her birth; for in that hour it is I who proceed from the side of the dead Savior; it was upon me, for my sake, looking toward the gifts that would be mine in my own time, that the Spirit descended on Pentecost."

As the Church's unity makes of her one Body now, one in rule, one in faith, one in the sacraments and in grace; so her apostolicity traces a long line backward through time, forward in time; at any given moment, from the instant of her creation, she was the Church of Christ; she knew it, she declared it; and her fullness of self-knowledge guaranteed for all her members, those militant, those suffering, those in glory, those yet unborn, an inclusion by the love of the Trinity, in the Mystical Body of the Savior.

What are the links of men today with the apostolic past of the Church? It might be well to pause for a moment on the effect which any tradition has on the present. A healthy attitude toward the past will always respect it without being enslaved by it. For a certain mentality it is always easy to praise a thing if it is far enough removed; to find only good in the past, and only defects in the present. But such an attitude is not only unhistoric, implying as it does that imperfection is a modern invention; it is also supremely unrealistic, in the sense that it refuses to discern a tendency in man, imperfect certainly, but continuous and evident, toward his proper good. The whole sense of the past, if it is to make any sense at all, is its living connection with the present, its impact on action and institution now, the way it exerts leverage on present effort. One must be willing to recognize (and this is a form of humility) that there are no canonizations of the human; in the sense that certain ideal forms have finally been achieved to write finis to the search for the beautiful, or the politically best, or the supremely useful. This, it would seem, is merely good sense on any plane, for non-believer or for Christian. If it is poor sense, then the men of the present were simply born too late; man is progressively reduced to a spectator's role in a world of museum pieces.

But if the text of past greatness can be translated at all, it will read: available for the present. To see life as a continuum; the larger is one's immersion in history, the more is one able to discern pattern and form and order, to arrange the discontinuity, the surface chaos of the present. There is a kind of natural "apostolicity," as old as the history of man, which uncovers and evaluates and uses the substratum of goodness and beauty that has moved imperceptibly in the direction of the present. Thus the meaning of the whole race is realized in the present, in the men who contain within themselves now, by largeness of horizon, by a historical sense, the whole past of their race. This breadth of man facing his past is only a larger self-consciousness: one would certainly weaken the term if one were to reduce it to the awareness or reactions of the soul to its present experiences. It is truer to say that conscious man discerns himself as a meeting place, a point of juncture, for all time; in him are summed up past and future in a present which waits to serve his choices, his own achievement.

How much longer, how much richer, is human life when man views himself as summing up all men, a threshold upon which history meets and grows eloquent; when he sees that in recapitulating all men, he has really summed up the created universe; since whatever worth matter is to possess, it will gain by its assimilation to man! Man is in the truest sense the whole universe grown conscious of itself. The purely material order with its seasons, its enduring and living forms, its material species, all the tools and riches buried within it—these are impoverished and provisory; they await the coming of their master. And when his hands and genius rest upon them, reflect upon them, draw relations between them, conclude from their nature to their Creator; it is at this point of time, whenever it occurs, that the material universe can claim to have begun the process of its own achievement; a process of humanization, the service of man.

Now, to speak of man's link with the past of the Church is really to claim for him once more a bond with the past of all men. The past of the Church is not apart from the history of man; it is that very history viewed from the eminence of the Divine plan. Man's first link with man in the unity of the origin of the race was not destroyed or imperiled by the new link of a supernatural destiny; the second has strengthened and guaranteed the first. So the function of grace as a completion of nature is illustrated again; birth in Christ has given a new poignancy to unity in Abraham and Isaac and Jacob, renewed man's bond with Abel, and with Adam himself; the seed of these men is the race of man. And the greatness of these patriarchs does not lie in the biological foundations of a race, but in the new illumination of their history granted in their Son, the Son of their race, the Word Incarnate, and their glory in being types of Him.

So it is with the saints of the New Law; as renewal of the Incarnation and proofs of its power they prevent, in a very true sense, the fact of the Incarnation from being submerged in history; they render present once more an event which must live on into every man's present. Grace again reinforces a statement of common sense: Man does not know himself until he knows all men, until all men and all great events are made present to him by the breadth of his vital acts. So every man is the history of redemption made present, either in fact or in hope. The entirety of sacred history is set marching in the direction of the individual soul. In his acceptance, in that free and human act by which he welcomes the stirrings of grace, and receives the Person of the Son of God as his Life, the apostolic character of the Church is once more vindicated. The Risen Savior is again victorious.

So each man can say, from the moment when grace receives him; he is apostolic, he shares in the glories and the history of his Church. His links with her past centuries are so various, so significant, from both the human and the Divine points of view, that one can do little more than exemplify them briefly here. One of the most striking ways in which the Church expresses man's inclusion in the moment of her birth is the Mass. All that was done for her on Calvary is renewed with sublime effectiveness at the Mass; she is plunged again, with all her members, into the open side of the Savior; with this change, that the wounds of the altar stream now with light instead of blood; that she immolates in her priesthood a Savior of glory as an indestructible pledge of His faithful love. The living cords of Christ exert again and again their traction toward the Father. The Church enters His wounds and issues from them, at will; by His will, which is her own. And coming forth, she is always and again the bride without wrinkle or stain, the youthful one who, going to the altar of God, is forever renewed. From the altar she is present again at the one death of the Risen Lord; not as simple onlooker; but as lover, as friend, as fruit and term and firstborn.

So in regard to the members of the Church, it is the Mass that bears them back to witness the moment of their birth, to witness how God has loved them, to what depths His love was willing to go, the creative effect His love has had. Men that were born at such cost, what is their true worth? How will it ever be weighed, but in the blood of the Savior? At the Mass men learn again that first definition of themselves which God has proclaimed in the act of creating them to the image of His Son. God has named them here, a name which pride or unbelief or simple inability to submit before love would willingly erase; but He will not allow them to forget as long as the blood of the Savior rests upon the altar.

What is the name conferred on men there? "I have called you friends. . . ." They are again sealed as His children, the children of light, children of the alliance; they are members of His own Body, members whose most secret tissues His sacred blood visits and inebriates; admitted again to paradise, to the presence of the tree whose fruit is His Son; children welcomed to the house built on a mountaintop, to the tabernacle of the most high. Born of Him, they bear His features into the bitter work of human life. Born of Him, they are compacted of those desires which animate Him forever; the eternal vision of unity, the salvation of all men.

But it is not only the Mass which links men with the whole massive and cosmic history of the Church. The sacraments are stages on the road toward a full maturity in Christ, and therefore in her. The man who has been baptized has entered the Church, and into him the Church has entered. His history is now passed from a profane to a sacred one; it is compounded of her own; he will from henceforth have nothing to hope for; no destiny; no future, no present, no past, except her own. He has wedded her, with a promise of absolute and eternal fidelity; by a love that is faithful and fruitful the Church and he have exchanged their vows; he has renounced the past to accept her past; he has renounced an individual destiny to accept to the heart all the responsibility, the anguish, the glory which her corporate life implies.

IV

All Things New

How can one make hunger for the truth, for a knowledge of things, of men, of "event," one with the hunger for God? The question is a capital one, for the stake of the Christian in his world is very great; he is to find his fulfillment in a vocation which demands that he take creation seriously.

On the other hand, Christian asceticism implies a most rigorous detachment from the world, from "creatures."

Between these two poles, of a lifelong constant dependence on creation and the most demanding and daring independence of it, the Christian works, prays, suffers, and wins his eternity. Is the synthesis his faith demands of him too daring to be realistic? A few reflections may illumine these areas.

For the Christian, knowledge and love of creation is one inseparable act. Perhaps it would be good to consider love and knowledge as a single phenomenon, and to unite what scholarship has been at pains to distinguish for so long. In order to be worthy of the name Christian, knowledge of the world must become progressively "real," in Newman's sense, by a loving contemplation.

Indeed, does one really ever know anything he does not love? It could be doubted. By knowledge, man enters creation; but by love he assimilates the world to himself. And the process must be unified, if knowledge is to have acuity, if love is to transform. For if knowledge gives man the other, love gives him over to the other; into experience of a reality that is not a mere counterfeit of himself. Together, knowledge and love, as one vital act, surround, penetrate, and synthesize reality.

Some precisions are immediately in order. Along with the gift of self to creation, there must be admitted to the soul a purifying process; men being what they are, the world being ambiguous. Otherwise, man is in proximate danger of setting up the world as a monstrous pantheon in its own right. A potential complicity exists between the wound in man's nature and the provisory nature of all things; and when man meets his world in a love which reserves nothing, a corrupting process can easily be set in motion.

And how is one to achieve this spiritual poise, a love for things which does not destroy? Perhaps the mind of the saints is the rule here, for a use of creation that will not only be ascetically safe, but will heal and correct and guide man's attitude toward creation; which in the Creator's intention would seem to be a wonderfully potent instrument for the perfection of the Mystical Body in time, through the action of man upon his universe.

One cannot help noting how, under grace, the saints attained a kind of instinctive right judgment in the use of things. They came finally to use creatures infallibly in relation to God; without deviation, scruple, sensuality, with a holy sense of the cross, utterly liberated. Life for them became a dialogue between the Holy Spirit indwelling them, and the Holy Spirit manifesting Himself in His creation. Before the glance of the saints, that creation seems momentarily freed, even for the onlooker, of any corruptive element; the saints restore a paradise all around them. In the dialogue of creation, the Spirit names creatures as His own, as holy, as images of Himself; and the soul, because it has for so long grown resonant with His presence, makes a vital descent into creation, without danger or violent effort. Simply, the saint sees God in all things.

He sees, that is, as a single vital action of knowledgeable love, or of loving intuition, the Triune God at work in the work of His hands. The Father is in labor with continuing creation; the Son, as active and single Exemplar of all things; the Holy Spirit, releasing through time the energies of the Risen Savior into the Church which is His own Body.

And this intuition of God in all things is the Christian's habitual attitude; it marks the high point of his ascetical effort intersecting with his mental life; an aura of the Divine Presence about one's labors, prayer, death: to see God at work, in all situations and enterprises of life, through man advancing His definitive victory. To see God at work, showing such respect for His creation, that He labors in and with it, manifests Himself in it, is concerned that its image of Himself endure and grow; so He curses the sterile tree, the idle rich, the hidden talent, the hangers-on in the market.

The Christian's choice to enter the world of things has no alternative; Infinite Knowledge and Love became incarnate in His world. He willed to embrace, in an experimental knowledge, and with a human heart, His own creation; to subject Himself to the lesions of time and place; all the circumstances that define human life. And this Knowledge and Love of men expressed Itself, in a plenary sense, on Calvary. Here, Knowledge and Love were infinitely fruitful; out of creation they created the Church, and began an endless generation of Divine fecundity, conferring in the sacraments the power to create men and women to His image to the end of time. God's knowledge and love were also divinely accurate: they defined the world forever, in a single act; and defined it in the act of transforming it. So it is only the dying Christ (and the Church issuing from his side, and therefore knowing His Heart and Mind) that can give a definition of the world: potentially, at least, the Body of Christ.

So the Christian's knowledge and love of creation is sanctified in a plenary act. In two ways, chiefly: by adhesion to the Church the Christian acknowledges that outside the Church man can never really know or love anything in truth; himself, the world, time, events, all remain peripheral isolated phenomena. But what the Christian is given through the Church is Paul's vision, a recapitulation of all things in Christ, the inclusion of himself and his world in reality.

And the second great fact that sanctifies the Catholic's love and knowledge is the Mass. Here man knows himself in the act of being transformed; and receives by faith a new definition: branch, spouse, redeemed friend. With the permanent redemption perennially at his disposal, man learns his own name and destiny, and becomes prophet of the truth to all of creation. He comes to love others with a transforming love, a love that would generate sons to God and restore the order of service and submission to the universe.

For at the Mass, material creation is caught up into the uses of the Body of Christ; bread and wine become symbols of the Divine implication of all things; there is literally nothing in life that falls outside, that evades this scrutiny of grace, the uses of love: to remake, to redeem. So in these two, union with the Church and union with the Mass, the complex of love and knowledge takes root and grows in human life, producing that most unlikely triumph: the saints. And through them, the text "I am with you all days" receives a new impulse; for the Spirit reveals Himself not only in the presence of an incorruptible body of truth, but in the witness of holiness as well.

To return to the original question: How can one make his hunger for creatures one with his hunger for God? One possible answer would insist: The use of creatures becomes an act of the love of God when creatures are subjected to the synthesis of Revelation. Man enters and possesses the natural world, events, when he sees them all undergoing and contributing to the action of the Word Incarnate, mediated by the Church.

And what is this action? First of all, a process of gradual self-revelation. Nothing in the world can escape the gaze of the Church, which is the Mind of God, focused through all ages, on His works. The New Adam gives a "name" continually to the world, because the world is given over to the Church; the type of her task was Adam in the garden: to release, by his contemplative presence and his love, the image of God in creation. The Church knows that only the Holy Spirit can name with accuracy the works of His hands. In the highest sense, this "naming" of things amounts to the performance of the Church's daily acts—the practical signs of grace and the Sacrifice; she "names" this as My Body, and it is done. In the sacraments, she names water, oil, salt, formulae as her own, drawing them aside from their natural context; a magnificent derangement of nature by grace, and at the same time an unparalleled use of creatures, a generous acceptance of what is in fact her own.

And from the altar, her naming of things goes outward into possession of the material world. There is nothing worthy of human life upon which her blessing does not rest: the fruits of the fields, modern inventions, tools of work and recreation, workshops, homes, city and farm buildings. Through her the area of the sacred is marvelously advanced, until man in his toil and prayer and hours of relaxation can see the smoke of adoration rising from his hands, and all the areas of life become an extension of the altar of sacrifice. So the Church makes the world into an instrument of the mystical renewal of her members, declaring with the calm voice of the Creator: Nothing is secular save sin. Through these creatures, elevated to her uses and the use of her members, the whole world becomes liturgical, and is drawn into the great hymn of adoration that ascends formally from her consecrated sons and daughters. Surrounded by the vestiges of God's love, her men and women are born again, nourished, undergo the Passion, and attain glory. It is the Mind of the Church at work, in no abstract or magical sense, but in a true assumption of creation to her heart; an assumption that reminds men continually of the Incarnation, and the Divine respect it implies for their nature and their world.

So the Church's naming of creation, her effortless knowledge of it, is one act; and the act, as every vital act, is transforming; it brings about the marvelous exchange of the human and the Divine in time, the exchange between time and eternity, the daring action of eternity within the confines of time. The Church knows the world only by creating the world anew, by redeeming, sanctifying it, by revealing herself as Mediator of the Trinity in time, generating the world to the Divine Features, opening the portals to Redemption and glory, herself invitation, means, and goal. What is not known by her, and still lives? Who is named by her, and not saved? Hers is the only intelligence that can fall with splendor, power, with a sense of possession and redemption on the whole of creation, and the least members of it. On time and eternity; on the universal Plan, and the mysterious Cause; the only love that really accomplishes, that is itself relieved of all trace of the temporal, the expedient, the selfish; and in its secret action, makes all over to its own image.

Now it is true to say; what the Church does, her members do, since they are in fact herself. The members are called to know, love, possess the world. St. John of the Cross: "The heavens and the earth are mine, the flowers are mine, and the seasons; the stars, the days and the nights . . . because Thou art mine. . . ." Through Christians, the indwelling Spirit brings the world to its knees in adoration, in ordaining it to the uses of Redemption. There is literally nothing outside this synthesis; the Spirit claims all, possesses all, and His action is accomplished through human mediators, knowing and loving the world by His principle, grace. And of these mediators, the saints above all know the world for what it is; because they have heard its identity whispered to them by the Church's Spirit, Who is their own. And what is this name whose resonance has reached their hearts, so that their lives strove to share its good news? It is, in regard to men, the Pauline word Body: in the word of Christ, Branch and Vine; the Canticle's Spouse and Beloved. In these words the Spirit reminds humanity of that one Form to which all must be gathered. With regard to natural creation, the Spirit names things as instruments to invigorate the Vine, to give delight and nourishment to the Spouse, to facilitate the task of the Body. The Spirit simply names all things as His own; sometimes in a most painful sense, as when a certain instrument is allowed to crucify the Body; or to aid It in attaining the full stature of Christ; all, even the wood of the cross, is ordered to the final glory of the members.

And the saint, hearing the secret name of creation which swings it wide in a vast unity of order, wisdom, love—hearing creation named and understanding its destiny—answers with a full acceptance involving him immediately in the supra-rational order of grace; involving his affections, energies, years, capabilities; his body and his life. His answer may bring him to Mary's work (behold the servant of the Lord) or in John the Baptist's (He must increase); in the Apostles' (leaving all things, they followed Him), in Simon of Cyrene's; in Zaccheus'; there is an infinite variety of responses to the call. But the response is a whole vocation; not operating in a vacuum, but welcoming creation into the world of grace in the company of all the redeemed; receiving and circulating life, counseling and accepting the truth, moving forward with all men to the Father.

Only the saint, to conclude, can love the world with any possibility of transforming it. The Divine principle of action within him continually projects itself, overflows, in a redemptive stream on the world. And in the area of use, he alone can be safely entrusted with the fate, the future, of creation; since he alone knows its destiny in the fullest sense, and is given grace effectively to fulfill it.

Some further reflections occur. Many things in creation are instruments of suffering; but grace has made them into instruments of the Passion. Before Christ, they could only torture a man; now they offer him eternity. They have a new virtue to communicate, and he a new power to receive it; so their presence keeps in motion the cycle of the Mystical Body after Christ; through the cross to glory. These things pierce the members, but in order to release life.

The idea of choice in the use of creatures falls rightly on quantity; but it should fall primarily on their quality; that is, their power to reveal the name of God to a man in a certain state of life.

Vocation is in a sense the central thing of all; it channels lives, ensures many correct choices as to the "quality" of creatures, and ensures illumination in the choices that remain.

Engagement is taking creatures to heart for the uses of the Church; attachment is using them, and being used by them, for any other reason; an aberration.

If Redemption had been effected without the cross, one could visualize Christian humanism, founded solely on Nazareth and the public life of Christ: a harmonious and undisturbed development of manhood toward the fullness of Christ, involving the "good life," an apostolate of great éclat, and so on. But Calvary is a fact; there is simply no other starting point for growth. Either one admits the Crucified to his prayer, study, psychology, or he ignores reality, and risks a life of illusion.

To know the world as the Church knows it; an ideal for the theologian, the saint, the artist . . . sharing her self-consciousness, which is inseparable from her love.

In a transcendent sense, it remains for the priest to make explicit the relation between the Word Incarnate and creation. Without the bread in his hands, there would be no renewal of the death of the Lord, no Body on our altars.

The creatures which offer a promise of glory on earth represent a great difficulty; are they always to be shunned as pure temptation? The Christian realizes they offer a false state, since there is no such thing as a definitive earthly rest. Safe use implies two principles— the glory creation brings a man (learning, reputation, honor) is to be referred to the glory of the Church, Head and members, and used in that direction. Again, one must constantly recall the true character of things. What they really offer is not vision, but a momentary transfiguration. Therefore, one must be ready to live independently of them, to go on with the business of life, deliberately indifferent to their presence or absence.

With regard to creation, the Christian is optimistic in the face of judgment. He knows the answer to the question: What of the laborious genius of art, science, literature, that through so many tortured centuries has risen to the stature of a common, treasured possession of man? It is good to recall that only the things Redemption has not touched will be excluded from eternal life. Judgment does not imply so much a holocaust as a division; the just will rise to glory, but the grandeur of humanity will not be stripped of the laborious human growth it attained on earth. Christ our Lord ascended with all His human years and memories, with that growth in wisdom and age and grace of which Luke speaks. The Mystical Body will know a glory conformed to His. It will know and love all things in God. Precisely as material, the creation it has used long and well will now be used up; but as objects of love and sources of knowledge, their existence, like that of the Body Itself, will not be taken away; it will only be changed for the better; *vita mutatur, non tollitur.*

One comes to "know creation" in many different senses: by a vast intellectual effort, by cataloguing, by reflecting, by reading, by taking a walk in a spring garden. Most efforts at knowledge are, as far as synthesis goes, centrifugal: they flee the center of things. Hand in hand with the most strenuous effort at knowledge, one must be willing to admit a synthesis effected by the Holy Spirit, the kind of wisdom which is so often the secret possession of the unlettered. Along with labor, study, dialogue, one must be content to be interiorly passive; to "do nothing and be still"; to be dealt with, to be labored over, by the Spirit Who has created and renewed the earth, and Who can alone reveal the true face of creation to man.

What direction does growth take in the man who encounters creation as a Christian? As far as one can predict (since grace is wonderfully autonomous, and smiles at formulae) something like this: A gradual independence of the temporal element in things. An easier, more instinctive reading of the Divine Presence. An easier transition from study of creation to contemplation of it; and in the latter, a growing simplicity of regard corresponding to its meaning, and the nature of the Spirit Who reads its text for man. And finally, "By the Holy Ghost, the soul arrives to offer God to God."

In the rhythm of grace, passivity always precedes God's action. Does not this principle reproach a tendency to force creation, by a violence of effort, ambition, haste—stifling the Holy Spirit, Whose Voice is so interior and secret, and Who alone can reveal His various manifestations?

In God's good time, all things.

V

Person

Many of man's judgments are only the sum of his experience. So he tends to limit reality to its immediate manifestations to him; to consider, as though it were definitive, only the measure of being that reaches his senses. So in achieving a notion of the person, one tends almost automatically to limit the person to a human composite. But immediately faith enters to correct and enlarge the idea; because angels are truly persons, and yet are purely spiritual; and God, faith and reason say, is a Spirit. So with the connection of the person and time. One instinctively grants the person forty or fifty years to place his mark on the shifty matter of the world; judgment tends in one's own case to make provision for only a limited number of active years; to expect, after that, the inevitable decline and falling away of powers, of those excellent gifts which are the property and expression of the person itself. But immediately a corrective judgment enters again; for all men are destined to live forever, persons in a state changed for the better; and of God the Trinity of Persons, personality at its absolute, one predicates eternity itself.

The case is parallel in the idea of the person existing and acting in space. One accepts the limitation: a corner of the world to work in; a certain number of men to influence through personal action. There is a necessary limit to the number of lives one can affect, even with the marvelous extensive power granted men in the new modes of communication. The suspicion arises sorrowfully that the more thinly the human person is extended, the less impact he can expect to exert in regard to those gifts called personal; the law of the person in time and space seems to be one of necessary limitation, both because of the shortness of life and because of the nature of a composite being. Yet faith hints that this judgment needs correction too; it hints at a larger possibility through multilocation; it teaches a kind of multipresence through believing prayer and the effects of the Mass; the persons of the risen, after the last day, will be gifted with agility; and the angels move, easily and at will, with the speed of thought; God is properly called immense because wherever creation exists He is present to it. He is nowhere because He is everywhere; all reality confronts His person; because He is, all things are; apart from Him is only nothing. And one is drawn to conclude that man can be present only to a certain number of men in the order of nature, depending on a necessary physical or moral proximity; but as the person is released into the purity of its destiny, limitations on the person are revealed as provisory, awaiting the correction of eternity.

Faith enters again into any consideration of the gifts the person has to offer: communication of himself to others; those activities of mind and will and emotional life which all men agree in naming great or worth while or permanent; the magnificent projections of the person in any field of endeavor; works of art, advancements in science, the development of dogma and philosophy. With all of these, a law of limitation surrounds the intellectual and the artist. No matter how marked with originality or breadth these things be, they are nothing more, in a sense, than the accidents, the part; man gives the word and retains the mind; he gives his love while retaining the will to love. But with the Trinity of Divine Persons, the notion of personal gift is again marvelously enlarged. The Father conceives the Word Who is His own substance; He gives Himself, and His gift is another Person, equal from eternity to Himself. And the Father and the Son love each other from eternity; and their love is a Person; and faith concludes: person at its height does not give merely the lesser part of himself. Person that Is, is a complete sharing, an emptying without exhaustion, the gift of the Giver in His totality.

Again, considering the work of man in time, one arrives at another painful conclusion. The community life of man, the sharing of personal gifts is ringed around with effort, labor, loss, with depletion of those resources the person rejoices to have at his command. Examples are too numerous to need recalling: the exhaustion of artistic effort, the weariness that follows a strenuous concentration on an object of love; the bloody entrance which knowledge forces, the necessity of sleep, recreation, distraction to rupture an unbearable continuity of mental effort. Wisdom and love are won at immense cost; a cost of precious time, of labor, of psychic energy. No human person can work for any length of time, at his peak; what one notes in the lives even of the great are certain isolated moments, flashes of lightening across their landscapes, gathering of power into a concentrated brief occasion of effort and achievement. The person must struggle toward one brief hour when his genius will vindicate itself in a work that distills all of life and illumines existence. But until that hour, and after it has passed, he undergoes the harsh pedagogy which tells him most painfully all he is and all he is not.

The artist and the saint, most of all, achieve personality at a cost that will never be fully paid, an exaction always at hand, the deed of art, the deed of love; men wonder at the achievement, and warm themselves at its fires; but the harsh truth remains, marking greatness with the human wound. It would be perfect, or not at all; but in fact it is imperfect; it is next to nothing. The same eye which brought it into being now judges it; and the judgment is harsh in proportion as the effort was pure: How will history judge it? How does God judge it? Those persons who live at the finest point of the person are those who win from the same painful vantage a humility which is simultaneously glorious and afflicting. To be the person, to act as the person, to give a new definition of the capabilities of the person, to be discontented with formulae of how much one can accomplish, to assimilate the world as though it had just left the hand of the Creator, and was still awaiting, vibrant and unexplored, the regard of man upon it; the task is clear. One must be the first of men, the first to love, the first to dare to create; and in that originality he will know at the heart: In this act I have depleted myself; I have suffered a lessening that time will not renew; or, I have loved, but a gaze of unbearable purity is upon that love; in comparison with It, the love of man is less than dust: for in the very act of love, if it is authentic and honest, a voice sounds: I am the One Who is, you are the one who is not.

But faith enters again; a simultaneous corrective and consoler. There is another form of existence, into which certain creatures have entered already, and which man may tranquilly await in hope. For the angels are constituted in a wonderful completion, a perfection of the person. They know and love with a fullness, an ease of action, a total expression of their personality, a regard that does not grow old or wearied. And the Blessed Trinity, finally, is infinitely removed from time and trouble, altogether achieved in Itself, giving and knowing, sharing and receiving in the shoreless sea of Its own fullness; the Three Persons saying from eternity their I am, I know, I love. And the conclusion: person at its height has within it the full flowering of eternity, perfection, light, knowledge, love, communication. "All Thy possessions are mine; all my possessions are Thine."

Again, in the idea of the person the notion of the incommunicable is often stressed. Perhaps as a reaction against the terrible invasions worked upon personality by modern life, man likes to remind himself of the hard encystment nature has placed around him; a spiritual guard of mystery, of self-possession and spontaneity. When the person enters a community, it is true that he normally grows more surely by a new rhythm of gift and use; but he always retains the inviolate center of personality to himself. Even in the highest sharings of the person known to man, the personality itself remains shrouded in mystery and self-keeping; the bride is never possessed in any radical sense; the friend remains forever another; what is offered can be withdrawn; the communication can end, and end in a deliberate isolation. The person retains himself, with the choice always at hand to demand back what it is possible to give at all. But with person at its height, the notion of totality and permanence in sharing are the reality itself. The life of the Person within the Blessed Trinity is necessarily a community life. "I am in the Father, and the Father is in Me." A unity of persons in God would be monstrous; a Father without a Son would empty the name Father of all meaning; a Father and a Son without a Holy Spirit would be a God without love. The Holy Spirit would be unintelligible apart from the Father and the Son, for He is the Procession of Living Love, Each for Each.

So men of faith are justified in concluding: The excellent work of the Person, of Person at its height of realization, is perfect knowledge and perfect love: such knowledge and love as eternally and of its very nature, generates, spirates, communicates; is fruitful, filial, is a consummation. But what is the most excellent work of the Trinity with respect to men? It is that act of creative knowledge and love through which was decreed the manhood of the Second Person of the Blessed Trinity. For the human race, the surpassing work of the Trinity was the gift of the Son to be truly God—with us.

Now this involved many changes; not in God, but in the human person; in his condition in time, in his status with regard to God: in the approach to the Father he now enjoyed; in the power of prayer made in the name of the Son, in the riches one could claim of Him. For the Son, only-begotten with respect to the Father from eternity, becomes in time the Firstborn of many brethren. Men have now what theologians call a new relation to God: they are become what St. Paul mysteriously calls the Body of Christ. They are assimilated to what St. Augustine names the total Christ.

The greatest work of the Trinity with respect to man is the human nature of the Son of God. But the vocation of the Word Incarnate is prolonged in the Mystical Body of Christ. So to conclude: regarding the Incarnation in its whole effect and intention, one may say: under another aspect the great work of the Blessed Trinity is the Church, the whole Christ, the Good Shepherd and His flock, the vine and its branches.

What difference does the new membership in Christ, this being grafted to Him, make in one's notion of the person? What corrections does faith grant here? One must speak, in every direction, of a marvelous strengthening, release, deepening of the person's ontological status, of his effectiveness, of his vision of history, of his destiny. The person, after being joined to Christ, is truly the same person; but he is just as truly no longer the same. He is on a different road; he has new aids, his outlook is radically elevated; his vision is enlarged, his companionship fortified. He is now part of a new community, such as has never existed before under the sun. When he encounters another member of the Body, each is recognizable to the other by faith as bearing the features of the Son before the heavenly Father. Being members of a same Body, these persons share a common bond which strengthens friendship and mutual presence, grants them a deeper sense of fraternity, of common action and common aid.

No person is alone in the old, destructive, vitiated sense of the word. There are no closed systems in the Body of Christ. Personality has no bars up, no locks at the door. Each member lives by the same life as his brother, each shares the same riches of the Father, each can say: I am greatly loved by the One Who has loved you. Each can say; Because of Him Who loved me, and delivered Himself up for me, I love you and deliver myself for you. Each is one of the many brethren of whom One is the firstborn. Each is engaged manfully in time for the sake ultimately of a communal eternity. Each has a stake in the destiny of all the others, for of every one will be demanded on the last day: "Where is thy brother, for thou art his keeper?"

One can even say: Each is member of the other, limb for limb, in one Body; through the baptism which has given them a common entrance into the kingdom. They are one in the forgiveness of sin, in which the merits of the one Christ are applied to all who sorrow for their sin and are absolved. They are one in the breaking of the one sacred Bread: Augustine says, "Just as from many grains of wheat is made the same bread, and from many grapes is crushed the same wine, so from many sharers of the bread and wine, the Mystical Body is strengthened unto unity."

Another question: What can the person accomplish now, after being joined to the Body? Men are familiar with those magnificent projections of the person on human history, in the works of genius which are the glory of our race: Shakespeare, Michaelangelo, Homer, Milton gathered the universal into a supreme experience, with passion and such permanent effect that time only reinforces the original judgment of admiration and recognition. A few men leave their mark: a monument sunk so deep in men's consciousness that the last day will see it standing.

But for the majority of men, the mark they make is pitiful indeed. All is vanity; man is grass; was the old threnody of Jewish and pagan literature alike. One speaks habitually of the average person, the good person, the person who is not unusually intelligent or gifted or witty. Even when a man is praised for qualities that will make their mark enduringly, he is set against the thousands who will not. The person, as men judge him, is a feeble, anonymous instrument. His work is the victim of time. There are so many millions of graves, and so few who live on in the gratitude of others, or the pervading memory of greatness, or heroic tasks finished. There are few who are remembered, and fewer who are remembered with love. Some works of the person appear for a while enormously important, but only to the doer of them; or only because they have earmark of the present, vivid and fragile and momentary. But the characteristic of the human work that endures is necessarily its ability to withstand the judgment of time, which alone is capable of sifting dispassionately what is real value and what is merely a castoff or a phenomenon.

The order of grace faces men with a different situation. It can be stated ontologically, according to God's Plan; there can be no mediocrity in the men enriched by God's grace. There is nothing shabby or ordinary about the soul where the Holy Trinity makes its dwelling; which the Blood of Christ has cleansed. The person who can act in such a mode as to guarantee and strengthen his status as adopted son of the Most High God is fulfilling a destiny which binds him to the design of the Trinity and makes of him a meeting place for heaven and earth.

His actions, first of all, are capable of a fine independence of time. He is free of the hurly-burly, the inner chaos, the spiritual drying-up which characterize the natural man of action. He is marked by a quiet possession of his own soul, a security under change; his motives have undergone the fixative of eternity, and he acts in the conviction that what he does reverberates elsewhere; that his deeds are recognized and remembered by Another, Whose judgments are infallible and merciful. So he is not preoccupied with honors or politics, the games of children in time, of children who demand winning scores and human approval. He can bury himself wherever God's work demands his obscure presence and staying power, because the Father Who sees in secret rewards also in secret. Detachment, wisdom, finely considered action are all characteristic of his mastery over time, his independence of any tyranny men would set over him; freedom of judgment, the ability to plan in and with the Church, which is perennial and has time even for hope; all the virtues are his which distinguish a soul whose center is in eternity.

Expansion through the cross is his ideal; the growth of the person through a willed death. Was any other theme more vigorously explored, or more courageously preached to the pagan world of Gospel times? It is this act of the soul's drama that most frequently encounters wonderment or suspicion, or the plainest type of opposition. But the persistence of the theme, as a substantial of Christianity, is a measure of the depth and height of that Person Who is the Church's Lord, the accuracy of His imaging of the Father; the cross reveals and conceals in human language the very "mind" of the Trinity: a will to love.

And in this way; all things are good, but not all equally so. Human culture is all to the good, and must be expected and blessed; the progress of men is examined sympathetically, and welcomed, as long as it is not a mere fraud, or an ambush for the soul. At the same time, while welcoming into Catholic fullness the things time has named good or great, the Church confronts the man of time, the man of this world, with the fearless words of the Master: "Take up the cross. . . . unless the seed die . . . I bring not peace, but the sword. . . ." And this, not as an arbitrary command made without merciful regard by a God of vengeance, but as a mystical postulate which is also fully human. She says: You will be yourself, but only in this way. Suffering in Christ is to save you from yourself. Without this experience, endured in and with his Lord, the person degenerates into a mockery of himself; a brutal overseer, a man incapable of purified judgment. He falls without rising into one or another of the multiple extremes which disintegrate the Christian balance: from strength to harshness; from charity to softness; from inner stillness to self-regard and neuroticism; from activity to interior turmoil; from prudence into fear of decision; from decisiveness to a sterile, inflamed justice; and so on.

But suffering is self-discovery, in the truest sense. One does not need to add that no reference is intended to spiritual nostrums which make of the plan of infinite Holiness a matter of ridicule for thinking men. When God acts, it is not at the level of temporal well-being; it is not to plunge man deeper into the morass from which he has already cried for release. What one must expect from a Divine visitation is precisely the unexpected; a violent overthrow of values; and a Kingdom, in which the only one who is not welcome is the one who has no will to enter. But once within, or even well on the way, some attitudes are discarded by the force of a new love, others are assimilated by a kind of superior and delicate tact; the presence of love makes all clear.

And from that time forward, the progress of the person through time is capable of a new depth of life, revealed in a thousand ways: the practical capacity for sacrifice, an astounding range of energies and enterprise; an unerring judgment which is able at a silent glance to distinguish the ephemeral from the real; the ability, finally, to recognize and do homage to love at every threshold. And this, constantly, through the cross. Were the example of the Passion of the Savior not enough, the apostolic witness from Paul and the early men of the Church is at hand; no apostle who is not a redeemer; and a sober, virile invitation, which is at the same time a fearful warning: take up the cross, fall to the ground and die, lose our life and find it. . . .

Self-discovery of the person through the cross; a fearful realism pervades the Gospel account, and the Master's commentary on the way His Father chose for Him. Preaching the cross without the experience of the cross is nothing; love without the will to pay for love is nothing; charity that proclaims without acting is useless; the person who would live the Christian life at the comfortable edge of that terrible vortex—he does not know himself, the Master warns; he risks losing all accurate knowledge of his Lord: He creates a questionable universe about him and stamps it as Christian; and, all the while, he is shunted to the side lines of life, a spectator instead of protagonist; the lifeblood of the Church seeks another passage; it no longer reaches his heart. Without suffering, no discovery of self, no accurate knowledge of one's identity or direction. It must be added immediately: no discovery of the neighbor. The best analogies of love are from life. And in living things growth is both vertical and horizontal, a double expression of the one impulse. And in the life of man, the same selfishness that chokes off a viable ascent to God suffocates that love of the other which defines man's very task on earth. Selfishness is the word; suspicion of a universe in which one's very destiny is placed in another's hands, and the other's in one's own. A universe in which the Lord deals subtly and constantly with the individual through his neighbor, in which God wears the face of the neighbor, and appears at one's door, every hour and every day, imperiously demanding: labor, alms, food, shelter—the catalogue of our pitiful human need. A universe in which the Lord insists: without the will to give, without alms, without an interior despoilment which enriches the other, without a love which strikes to the heart of this world's values and slays them; without these, every man is condemned to be stranger to the other, tool to the other, object of the other; at his mercy, at his convenience. Hell has moved close, for earth is its waiting room. It was in suffering that the community of love was created. God knew no better atmosphere in which to envelop the birth of the Church: "And they crucified Him there. . . ." When the race of men had reached its darkest hour, and the number of those fit to be called had been reduced, of all the world, to a handful; it was in the hour when coldness and rigor set His limbs and death edged to His side, God decreed: Let there be light. One must try to enter as nearly as love can bear him, into the depth of those antagonisms which God has reconciled in His Church; death and birth, blood and water; sin and creative love, the freedom of an absolute and interior gift of love, the appearances of hatred and anarchy; finally, and most triumphant of all, person and person. But the meaning remains; out of Calvary, community, interior healing, restoration of peace, an earth which again takes heart, to hope and believe; a world in which the person has a chance to survive the terrible passage into eternity.

VI
Task

"Let this be the supreme law of our love; to love the spouse of
Christ, as Christ wished her to be, and as He purchased her with His
blood" (Mystical Corporis). The Church is coextensive with the
dream of God; a dream embracing all creation; a hierarchic and redeemed whole, a unity. Paul gives this revealed plan a formula: "It
was His loving design, centered in Christ, to give history its fulfillment by resuming everything in Him, all that is in heaven, all that
is on earth, summed up in Him." This design of unity is of course
concentrated on the desires of God with regard to men: Paul continues: "In Him it was our lot to be called, singled out beforehand,
to suit His purpose, for it is He Who is at work everywhere, carrying
out the designs of His will: we were to manifest His glory." The
intention of God, then, is recapitulated in Christ; it is incarnate in
His person. And it is extended, without substantial change or diminution, to the Body of the Church, which may be accurately defined
as Christ, living and active, in time. The Church continues to project Christ in the world; and in Him, the loving design of the Trinity; she may repeat with confidence, "The Father works until now,
and I work." It is then with no transfer of love that the believer
turns his regard from the person of the Incarnate Word to the
labors, struggles, setbacks, triumphs of the Church; he is merely fol-

lowing the glance of Christ: "Behold the fields, white for the harvest." At this hour there awakens in the Christian a new intention of what it means to love Christ; for the love of a person for another does not live within a vacuum; it is a total sharing of interests, desires, a love which is one in intensity and scope.

So when one awakens to the reality of the Church and turns to her, he is forming an act of the love of God that is at once personal and total. In loving the Church, he is obeying the first and second Commandments, which are one; the love of God and the love of the neighbor; he is putting to work the hard, temporal business of loving God; a love that must be tested for sincerity against the love one is willing to show for what He loves. And love of the neighbor will be, according to the Gospel, the very substance of the judgment to be made on our works. "I was hungry, and you gave me to eat, I was naked and you clothed me . . ."

The finality of the sacraments at once intensifies and resolves the perpetual agony of the Church to be realized everywhere, to be bound by no frontiers, to live in all men. Baptism is a bond of union, and a responsibility; it raises the soul from death to membership in the community of love; and, conferring life, it confers on the soul all the responsibility of new life; not mere existence, but the power and duty of self-reproduction; this is inferred in the rite of the sacrament: "If thou wish to enter life, keep the commandments; thou shalt love the Lord . . . and thy neighbor as thyself." From that moment there is no such thing for the Catholic as a selfish life, a life alone, a life of private orientation; he is swept up as a living member, into the designs, the finality of life itself; he is given the ends of the earth for his horizons, and a mandate, according to his station, to act as a bearer of life. The same vision is opened on the soul at Holy Communion. Being in union with the Head, the Catholic must at the same time open his eyes to the whole Body: he receives not a dead Christ, not an indifferent Body, but the Christ Who is still committed, still involved by reason of His glorious wounds, in the wounds of His militants upon earth. In glory, the Head looks to the eternity which will consummate the labors of all: and at the moment of Communion the soul that is awake will hear the cry of the total Christ; a cry of immense desire and triumph, of anguish and fulfillment; a cry that unites in a challenge and hope all the sublime disparates of time and eternity, of labor and vision, of bloodshed and glory. It is the cry St. Augustine speaks of:

What is this that cries from the ends of the earth? Who is this one Man who reaches to the extremities of the universe? He is one, but that one is unity. He is one, not in a single place, but the cry of this one Man comes from the remotest ends of the earth. But how can this one Man cry out from the ends of the earth, unless he is one in all? . . . the Body of Christ ceases not to cry out all day, one member replacing another whose voice is hushed. Thus there is but one Man who reaches unto the end of time, and those that cry are always His members.

There is, then, no possible excuse, in human life or at the moment of judgment, for not loving: God and the neighbor are the two finalities of the impulse of grace, finalities which are simply one. "In the evening we will be judged by love." And of all the Catholic complex of grace, the sacrament of union, the Eucharist is the great means for drawing the Christian community together; member to member, and members to Christ; allowing them to hear in the secret places of their heart the cry of the whole Body for union with Jesus, their common love; and eventually changing this anguished need into a silence of love, an embrace of glory. It is this sacrament which heals distances, dissolves differences and points of irritation, inflames the whole Body with the ambitions and desires of the glorious Head, and in the midst of the most anguished combat comes with a voice of absolute assurance and peace: "It is I: fear not."

It would seem that the Holy Sacrament today has a special grace in opening man to this cry of the Church Augustine speaks of. This is a magnificent grace of the present century; a new self-consciousness of the whole Body in regard to itself. The Church holds up the mirror of the Eucharist, and sees in it its own glory, extension, potentiality. When was the Mystical Body more conscious of its identity, its communal effort, of the need of heroism in all for the sake of each? One can see this awakening as the fruit of the decree on frequent Communion of some fifty years ago. Other significant reforms like those of the Eucharist fast, the Holy Week liturgy, the concern of the Holy Father that the Church worship intelligently, as a family—all these are means by which the Church realizes more exactly the pattern of adoration given us in God's Son; transformation in Christ to the image of the Father. And the transformation is a process individual as well as social; no one is lost or submerged. St. Paul is at pains to stress how the function of each member is retained, is regarded with a supreme respect for its natural and supernatural gifts in the work of the Mystical Body; it is not a question of a homogeneity, of a least denominator. "If the whole were only one single organ, what would become of the body?" Diversity is to be retained and perfected, since the whole body is in need of the operations of each member, cannot operate harmoniously and effectively if one is maimed or useless. . . . "The eye cannot say to the hand, I have no need of you, or the head to the feet, I have no need of you."

But Paul intimates that the Christian is what he is only in relation to the Body which receives, governs, and transforms him. There are no exceptions to the law; every man is destined to the beatific vision to be achieved by the graces of the Church: there are no private choices here; as though one could declare, I prefer to follow my own destiny, to go another road. A member, by very definition, is related to a greater reality; is irrevocably attached, can be what it is only because it belongs, receives energy, direction, function, in harmony with the life or the organism. An excised eye or arm is no longer a member in any real sense; it is simply an amputation. What had been an object of beauty, when united with the whole body, when contemplated in proportion to it, becomes an object of horror when separated from it. In the Body of Christ, effort, love, prayer, sacrifice, salvation are a social effort. The organ on its own, the member separated from the direction and labor of the whole, is a cancer, a monstrous deviation. "No salvation outside the Body" means precisely all salvation within it; all salvation that is in fact achieved has come about by some relation to the Body, no matter how tenuous; the Body's lifeblood has reached out somehow; its thought has inflamed the soul, the name of Jesus which the Church repeats tirelessly in the world has reached it; that single grace which spells an eternal difference has grasped its heart and set up a response of love, no matter how inchoative or fleeting. The life of the Body has reached the member; it would be more accurate to say: the life of the Body has made a living member of that which was dead, discarded, without hope or destiny.

This constant reaching out of the Church toward all men might be called the task of the Body; not an added quality, depending on the free choice of each member; but an agonizing total thirst, a postulate of its very nature. The Church must grow. She is spared death in any radical sense by the Spirit of the Risen Savior, but she is not spared that momentary lapse from splendor and vigor which follows from the relaxing of her apostolic effort in certain times or places. While she lives in time, she can never declare, I have suffered enough, I have labored enough, I have conquered. She is never allowed the goal of the ancient Jews, at ease in Sion. Let her claim the city, the countryside is languishing; let her win a continent, the world is still unwon.

And her effort is not to be merely geographical. Even supposing for an instant that, numerically, the world were in her fold, and the nations at the feet of the Savior, her work would continue; it cannot be called finished until the secret hour, which is known only to the Father, when He will come to reward her and lead her to an infinite peace. In the meantime, assuming that the world was won, and still the end of the world had not come, what work would remain?

The fact that one poses the question means that one has not plumbed the depths of the Church's impulse toward full possession of man. Her task is not a matter of numbers, of census taking, of processions and full churches; these must remain approximations, always subject to the fearful scrutiny of the Father, Who alone knows the men who fulfill in truth the definition of Christian. In her desire to see Jesus reign, the Church does not resign herself to a certain number who are willing to stand up and be counted; what she is anxious for, quite simply, is the formation of saints, the possession of the secret last places of the soul by the Savior; the presence of witnesses in the world who live and love and work independently of adverse or favorable circumstance; the bringing forth of souls who will show back to the Father the features of His only Son.

The only sense in which her task can be called complete is this: some of her members have already achieved heaven. In her altars

are the bodies of her martyrs, those bones which alone of all creation
lie within the altar stones of her sacrifice, as a sign and reminder of
glory. In these saints her task has triumphed; they were totally penetrated by her Holy Spirit as by a most sacred fire; they preserved
in the world the knowledge of who she is, and witnessed that knowledge unto death. So the saints are a continual reminder that the work
of the Church will always be, in its highest achievement, a question
of quality; of bringing forth those who, in the Pauline sense, have
truly and fully belonged to the Body. All her lifeblood, effort, desire,
the reason for her being, was theirs; because they were the image of a
historic Jesus Who refuses to be absent from the world, and could
live in and through them: "I have risen and I am still with you." It
was they who said to the Body, in their submission to the Church:
I have need of you; outside you there is nothing for me; in you and
through you is all the possibility I have for a greatness which will
evade time, selfishness, sin. It was they who suffered in the suffering of others, who found pleasure when others were treated with
honor, and between the poles of suffering and honor tasted to its
bitter dregs the world's reaction to the presence of Jesus confronting it in them. Finally, it was they whose love for the neighbor gave
a historical continuity to the claim of the Body that it belongs,
organs and tissues and cells, to Jesus. It is certain that but for the
example of the saints, the evidence of the Holy Spirit in the Church
would suffer diminution; because they offered their bodies as temples
for the Spirit, their words and acts live on with such supremely human fullness; a tenderness, an integrity, a quality that even the unbeliever must admit to be genuine—the "good odor of Christ" diffused
in His Church.

All this is not to state that the Body of the Church is only coextensive with her saints. But the saints are the supreme example of
the Church's triumphant consciousness of her mission and power.
The saints are the Church at her best; they are the Church at her
most active, effective, accurate. They pass her identity over to the
world without distortion; they seize vitally upon the truth she
teaches, and they prove: it works, it is the only thing that works,
that changes anything for the better, that gives men their chance
for happiness, that saves them from the inner corruption to which

the world is such a tyrannous ally. In them live the Church's own characteristics; their lives and death only make sense because she lives in them, and works in them. Her unity; the sacraments have grafted them to herself, and the marvelous variety of their gifts has always taught how great is the power of a common lifestream, asceticism, love, to affect the world: "God has given us different positions in the Church; apostles first, then prophets, and thirdly teachers; then come miraculous powers, then gifts of healing, works of mercy, the management of affairs, speaking with different tongues, and interpreting prophecy. . . ." Her holiness lives in them; this raised them to the altars physically, so that their bones serve to bear the Church's chief Treasure, the Body and Blood of Christ; and they merited the eternal dignity because of a holiness her judgment has termed heroic. They were heroic in love of her; this defines them finally; and they loved her because she leads men, as they realized, to the final term of love, to the Holy Trinity. They are finally apostolic, because they form another unbroken chain of evidence, from the days of His life among men, concerning that Word "Who is life, what He was from the first, what we have heard about Him, what our eyes have seen of Him; what it was that met our gaze and the touch of our hands." A common witness, alike in heroism and doctrinal exactness, a witness evading rationalizations which would reduce their mystery to mere ingenuity or the persistence of a common ideal.

So the task of the Church is illuminated in them: to raise up saints, men and women according to the image of the Word Incarnate, Who is our way to the Father. And this is to be done, not by any reduction of the human to a characterless mass; not by preconceived, inhuman formulae; but by a living, interior assimilation of the life of Christ; so that whatever is various, attractive, valuable in human life shall be welcomed to the divine process, and still shine forth clearly in the man of God. A synthesis, not a formula. The infinite holiness of Christ broken into its unending spectrum of values, virtues, activities. The history of the Church becomes a lucid text of the respect of God for the human in its progress toward Himself; Christianity would have been only a repetition of the various pagan systems if it supposed that man could escape himself or his condition, could evade time, could ignore responsibilities to his neighbor in the search for God. But the Catholic way is at once more complicated and more simple. It proposes nothing less than a daring attempt to work with the human, to work in time; to seek holiness not in conformity, the pressing into a mold; but to fill the interstices lying between the greatest human variety of talents and character; to unite them all in the generous fullness of grace; so that nothing truly human or valuable lies outside her ambit. Unity in Christ defines the greatest possible term of the human, because the full meaning of the Church's task lies in the figure of Him Who united literally in his Person all possible dimensions: the human and the Divine, time and eternity, the material and spiritual worlds, creation and its Creator.

The supposition is that as one regards the task from the interior vantage point of faith, he will retain a mind that is larger than its own ideas; a willingness not only to act, but to grow and to be led. The task of holiness implies that holiness itself, while a fact, is also a process in the Church; that an achieved equilibrium between the divine and the human is a definitive possession only in heaven; and that while on earth holiness is a journey, a perilous process. In time, the vessels bearing the Treasure will always be "fragile." And a constant temptation to the Christian will be to dispense with healthy fear and humility, the willingness to learn, submit, and suffer; to take his stand outside time, outside the task; the status of judge. It is always possible to piece together, from this or that section of the Gospels, a formula for holiness, social or personal, that will be only another form of selfishness, that will mirror the ambitions of nature instead of correcting them by the wounding impact of the Redeemer's truth. To act in this way is to stand outside the freedom promised by Christ; it is to introduce oneself, or others, only into a new form of tyranny, to lead prisoners only into another prison yard; more spacious, perhaps, but still hemmed in by insurmountable walls.

But the way to the life of Christ is by a death. The mind of Christ, if embraced in sincerity, impels one to enter by the narrow way. And that mind, in all its Divine fullness, implies the gift of itself, for others, even to death.

Christianity is the possession of eternity; it is victory, it is the expansion of the human, but under the dolorous conditions of time; in the here and now. Between the vast poles of those opposites, death and new life, suffering and joy, setback and hope, the Christian labors, without diminishing the fullness of the Catholic vocation. Eternity is one thing; it is not present to men except in hope; the task is one of this time and place. To seize the rewards of eternity while living in time would be, not the Christian task, but a "robbery," a "rapine." The lover of Christ does not seek the privileges of grace attached to eternity; he seeks its responsibilities; he is not dreaming of the thrones of Israel; he has at heart the human process of the Son of God, Who "came among us as one who serves"; Who "despoiled himself and took the form of a servant." In full liberty, He Who was rich emptied Himself, that by His poverty we might be enriched. To renounce, for the interim of life on earth, the prerogatives of glory: here is the Pauline formula for the Mystery, manifest to us in Christ, not as an object of admiration or wonder merely, but as a very structure of life. So the Christian attitude reaches a synthesis at the most painful level, the human experience of God Himself; not acting a part in our midst, not regarding our condition out of curiosity or levity, not assuming a costume, but truly made one of us, experiencing to the depths of His Being how glorious and painful a thing it is to be man.

It is the completeness, the divine realism, of this assumption of the human, that strikes the Christian soul like lightning. The despoiling, the outpouring of the Divinity of which Paul speaks, did not come about merely because the Son of God took a human body; but because He took a body of poverty, of humiliation, of suffering. It was man in the depths of his abasement who won the love of the eternal Word. All of man, or nothing; whatever He did not assume He could not have healed. The "mind of Christ Jesus" to be put on by the Christian as his attitude in grace is implied in this: that the Son of God Incarnate freely renounced the conditions, the surroundings befitting His dignity, the adoring response of men, the permanent state, if one may so speak, of Divinity made apparent. Another way of saying that the Transfiguration was a mere episode in His life, not the permanent state of things as He dwelt among us.

Although He was the Lord of Glory, He did not appear to man as such; but simply, to take from His own lips the word of his abasement, as servant. Surrounding that sublime Figure were all the human circumstances: mortality, fear of death, vulnerability to corporal and mental suffering, the risk of being taken for granted, of being a scandal to the hardened; He was fatigued, hungry, homeless, and in want; and all this to such a degree that for His own protection and growth He had need, as do all men, of the gifts and the aid of the Father. It is perhaps necessary to insist that this despoiling of Divine privilege was not merely a matter of material circumstance: the fact that He was born in poverty, or worked for His daily bread, or faced the world with a body that was subject to death. That He took the form of a servant means, at its very heart; in this human being, Christ, was an attitude of service; it corresponded with the eternal will-to-share in the Godhead itself; in time, it was a permanent ingredient of His attitude toward men; and expressed itself corporally in this Body which man would recognize for brother. Servant: not the hireling, or the stranger, but the One Who submitted Himself for love's sake; submission to authority in obedience, submission in the gift of His time and attention and energy to the needs of men; submission even of the Divine wisdom by patience and kindness, to the slow pace, the blindness of those among whom He moved.

Now this submission of Christ is the very point at which the grace of Christ attacks human pride, and makes the man of time, the potential superman, the man for whom self threatens to become absolute, into the image of Son of God. At this point in man's determination to serve, and the simultaneous temptation not to serve, the battle line is drawn, and Christian conflict begins.

A history of lingering Christian affection surrounds the Pauline formula; self-abasement as the Christian life. St. Augustine tells movingly in his Confessions how he "was searching for the necessary strength, and could not find it . . . because I did not yet hold in my arms my Lord Jesus, the humble pupil of a humble Lord." And P. de Grandmaison is in the same tradition: "The assuming of Christ comes about by the abnegation of self, even to the extreme of the emptying of one's self: He dispossessed Himself. The infinite honors due to Him as Son of God, equal to the Father, Jesus renounces deliberately, and accepts the form of a slave, the condition of slave, pushing humility even to the lengths of death, death on the cross. To consecrate ourselves to serve, since He took the nature of a slave. Service is the very device of this shield. . . . But of course there are different sorts of service; one glorious, recognized, honored; another humble, painful, constant, harsh. Perhaps one should unite the two forms; that of the soldier and that of the slave, the spirit of the one and the abnegation of the other; to do the task of a slave, but with a good heart. Such was the service of Christ among us; and at all cost, the one who takes Him seriously must enter into this mind when he undertakes to serve God and to put on Jesus Christ. Otherwise, one's life is both comic and bitter. . . ."

But it is by the very abasement, by the wood of the cross, that the resurrection is made possible. Humiliation, the gift of one's life to God for others; this is the indispensable process of things; the task of time; but it is not the final term. The task is provisional; it does not define Christ in glory, nor the Christian arrived at His side. Though Christ is man forever, he is not slave forever; now His manhood enjoys in depth and height and breadth the glory that it once freely renounced.

From the cross to glory. Who will not see in the very cross the urgency of divine love, the material, tactile, visible proof of love? And a love which has arrived at the final depth of the gift of itself; the death cursed by Moses in the law, reserved by the pagans for the dregs of their society. "Beautiful and free" was the Greek chant in praise of their gods; but the God of beauty, the One of essential freedom, casts Himself into this abyss; by this supreme abasement He offers the Father a homage that heals, a reparation that wins pardon.

To celebrate this supreme act, to initiate the Christian heart into its own vocation, St. Paul leads man strophe by strophe through the great hymn of Redemption; a hymn which is the center of the Church's liturgy, and the juncture of her greatest mysteries; Good Friday to the Resurrection. The first theme, abasement, corresponds exactly to the second, the Father's acceptance and response to the glory offered him by His beloved Son. "Wherefore": the great link is forged, for Christ as for the Christian; no glory except through a death. "Wherefore God has given Him a name which is above every other name." Because He took the name and office of Jesus, Savior, now the name jealously reserved through all sacred history for the eternal God, crowns the work of Christ: the Lord. He is Sovereign over all creation; every knee will now proclaim, even from hell: Jesus Christ is the Lord; His is a name equal to the name of the Father. Now every act of homage rendered to the Son is a homage to the glory of the Father. So in the great acts of God effected in the body of His Son; in the state of servant, freely assumed for men, in His resurrection, the conferring upon Him of the honor which was native to Him from eternity—in these, the Christian finds his pattern for growth and action. The process of grace is not haphazard; it has an interior direction; it aims to reproduce in the soul the events which marked His appearance among us, and according to their original order; so that death, suffering, humiliation are the very conditions of glory.

The task of the Church continues: to win the Father's glance of love by reproducing men of her own task, which is the Savior's. And through the Savior's imperishable love she is able calmly to make an incredible pledge; because she is forming man to His image, the world continues to encounter the Savior in them; that Countenance which faced the multitudes in His life upon earth—in miracles, in the fearless communication of the Father's love, in death, in rising again.

VII

Suffering

The Church is deeply realistic in placing on men the demand that they suffer for her. In so demanding, she is not vulgarly applying a biological principle; the individual is not sacrificed for the common good, or for the survival or prospering of the "species." Simply, the Church can demand that men suffer, within her and for her sake, on the various stages of human life, because she is what she is: the continuation of the Savior in time. And as suffering was a prelude to glory for Him, so it is for His members.

This authentic call to suffering in the spirit of faith does not diminish or attenuate liberty; it does something much more radical, more fearful; it subjects liberty to a series of deaths as a condition for its expansion. It does not lead human life into a corner; but it demands that humanism be ready to include Calvary in its synthesis, as well as Nazareth; that humanism follow the Gospel cycle honestly to its conclusions, and that it forbid the heart to loiter along the way in this or that ephemeral Utopia. The call does not drug or amputate the senses, but teaches a new hierarchy of attitudes in which the senses will never be allowed to king it over the healing darkness of the life of faith.

To suffer for the sake of the Church, to suffer, in the deepest sense, in the Church; even, to allow the Church to be the instrument of one's suffering, to suffer by her—this is the living formula she dares present to the Christian as the very condition of his growth in the Life of Christ.

One thinks of the Acts of the Apostles, of the first witnessing of the apostles in the courts of Rome, of Stephen before his executioners; of apostolic journeyings, trials, shipwrecks; of St. Paul and the autobiography of the man of the Church which he sent unashamedly to his Christians at Corinth; rugged and delicate, the irreplaceable record of a great heart. All this was only the beginning. The fact is that the first men of the Church were marked by a common grace which has never abandoned the Church; which is constant through the centuries of travail and suffering, of success and setback. Perhaps it is possible to formulate a law of grace in regard to all great men; the nearer they arrive, by sacramental life and prayer, to an experience of God, the greater will be the expansion of will, the positive readiness, to suffer for the Church. Genuine apostles, from the first twelve onward, have never thought to seek exception to the law of the Gospel set down unequivocally for their reading: "Whoever will follow, will take up the cross."

The cross is taken up for the sake of the Church, for the continuing redemption, for the sake of men. The cross has not become less central, or been reduced to a mere symbol, because the Savior of the world has been taken down from it. He was taken down to make room for others that the Redemption might go on, that Calvary may never pass into history, that its mystery might be a continuing presence to the world, a shock, a reminder, the logic of the Father's will as He regards sin and weighs the price of eternal life.

That the true apostle be able to suffer, a practical love is demanded, clear-sighted and realistic. He never evades a present cross for the sake of, under the pretext of, a possible one. The cross that is genuinely redemptive is always the present one, the one that this day has offered, the one that humiliates and galls and weighs heavily now. How the New Testament accounts bring before the Christian this fine sense of the value of present suffering: false judge or betrayal, hunger and thirst, parting from friends, prison, scourging; what is now set before Paul is the thing that must be got through, is the thing that counts—for the Church. Otherwise his opportunity is lost; the added poignancy of a letter to his Christians because it was written in prison, the immediacy of an appeal to the passion of Christ because that death is operating now in Paul's own body, the spontaneous sorrow and hope engendered because he has not only preached, he has endured and stood firm for the truth.

But most significant of the forms of apostolic suffering is the Pauline "solicitude for all Churches." Laboring in one portion of the world, giving all one's energies and heart to this or that acre of the vineyard, does not close off the heart. The proudest name any apostle can claim is his name of Catholic; he is the universal man; the thirst of Christ is not isolated to his lips or throat; he feels it to the last fiber of his being. The reality of the Church universal has made him one with itself; he has its struggles and triumphs at heart; with him the Church is not a matter of geography, so that he feels his enthusiasm diminishing with the outward miles; but the Holy Spirit Who is the Spirit of the Church makes everything present to him. He does not ask the Church to "come to him," to reduce her greatness to the capacity of his ideas; but he is growing into her; and especially at the Mass he finds that the words fit the fact; that he is increasingly dissatisfied with any prayer or request that stops short of the needs of all the "holy Catholic Church." The only gesture that satisfies his call to adore God is the gesture of the Mass: which is the plenary embrace of the Crucified, "for the salvation of the whole world."

His solicitude, then, is the living and prudent unity of a discreet love. He realizes that there are only so many hours to a day, so many years to a lifetime; that the human body is an instrument of the soul's effort, not its enemy; that to accomplish anything, his love must keep itself within the bounds of a limited energy, must observe a rhythm of labor and respose. In the matter of work, as in everything else, his sense of the Incarnation is alive; that the Son of God, in taking a human body, contained His action within human limits, did not play superman among us.

Zeal for the Church, the expression of a love that of itself admits neither boundary or horizon—unless this is prudently guarded and formed, contained within the bounds of a good sense that recognized the human situation, what a risk to the good of the Church!

The pages of history are littered with the ruin of those who loved without prudence, who loved too humanly, who placed the center of judgment in themselves instead of in the larger reality they were pretending to serve. Suffering in the Church is in a true sense having the humility to dispense a divine gift in a human way. It takes the blows of being human, and is quick to sense the tendency to domination and arrogance that would make the call of the Father over into man's dispensation.

Perhaps it is worth lingering for a moment over the delicacy and beauty of this Catholic "balance"; all fire at core, all self-possession and calm at surface, the mind of the Savior which reaches others across the frail human bridge of a body; a voice to speak, friendship to win, hands to serve, the will, finally, to die for the flock. Men are to be won by men: God wills in a courtesy proper to His goodness, to need men. And in the long run, to need men who live and die after the pattern of the Savior; in obscurity, in labor, in charity unfeigned; who have recognized and distilled the apostolic essential from the bitterness of life; to serve, to be available, not to hoard the one unrepeatable gift—life.

Apostolic men, the majority of them, live and labor and die upon the ordinary human stage: "not many great, not many noble, not many rich." And this even in regard to qualities of mind and heart, to that degree of greatness which projects men into public attention. To consider the men and women of the Church is to be struck by the radiant presence of the apostolic essential and, by and large, by the absence of any noteworthy human gift. A discreet love says everything; both terms must be fully weighed; a love which is an adherance to Another, through all the vicious or favorable tides of life. A love which is impatient of formulae, and embarrassed under their promulgation. A love which has been steeped to the core in the necessity for sacrifice, until the call to sacrifice stains its thought, as the color red stains the substance of blood. A love which the ancillary virtues accompany, so that all things are simply in place; purity, honesty, integrity, peacefulness of heart, intentness on God, so that the impression is unmistakable on anyone serious enough to seek, that a synthesis has been reached at the depths of the person, where the mystery of grace invades and permeates the mystery of man.

But a love which is ordered, contained, given its form and tone of service, by its careful adjustment to the needs of the other. The love which would move into action merely by whim or caprice or instinctive moods would be only another blind for selfishness. The one loved is always the measure of the truest love: the needs of the other, holy discretion toward the other, a fine tact and sense of time and occasion determine always the expression of love, its intensity on this or that occasion, the words or silence which will envelop it. The lover is filled, heart and mind and emotion, with the form of this loved "other"; in serving him he is serving another self; the consciousness of the other impinges so directly on him that he is able, by a kind of holy instinct, to divine the least unuttered whisper of need, of desire, of the call to response.

"Let this mind be in you which is in Christ Jesus." The implication seems clear. Love for Jesus Christ, apprehended truly in His Church, directs to a nicety of detail motive, hidden desire, ambition, emotional coloring, the whole process of love which is the Christian definition of life. A fine discretion in such love comes to this; that the ultimate weighing of difficult, crucial decisions no longer lies within the ambit of "nature"—but is assumed into the structure of grace; in effect, into the realized presence of the Beloved. *Sentire cum ecclesia*, that proud and sublime phrase, thus becomes the fulfillment of an apostolic love which would "put on Christ Jesus," would have in the sons of the Church "that mind which is in Christ Jesus." And the last word of love is a simple one: service. Solicitude for the Church; a fiery zeal content in time and in the body, because it holds suspect any triumph which would bypass the mystery in which it lives. What is most real in the Church is also most mysterious; the expansion of the life of grace in men, known only to the Father. All effort to communicate this life shares the same mystery; at its deepest it can never be the subject of human judgment. To labor for the mystery while awaiting its revelation: this is the apostolic mind.

The apostle will realize, then, that his truest point of entrance into men lies not in his directly human effort, but in those means of grace God has set up independently of him. His thirst is at once refreshed and increased at all the great sources of grace—especially at the altar. From that eminence, the fragments of the world interlock and attain a meaning; he is at the axis of reality; he is armed now, to act, to be truly effective. Whatever he could not do in a human sense, whatever evades one man or one lifetime, is marvelously extended and released; he draws out of eternity the nourishment that will renew the men of his lifetime. Here his "solicitude for the Church," his positive will to labor and suffer for souls, is freed from the danger of impatience and querulousness, of discouragement, of the human. The act of Redemption reminds him again, by the shock of its renewed presence, of exactly what he is trying to do for men: to redeem them through the death of Christ. Enlightened and purified in this way, his labor will never stop short at any halfway point of life; of ministering to a short-sighted justice, of saving the body at the expense of the soul, of allowing men to take root in the world. All the temptations that would infect the apostle with the poison of the merely temporal are cauterized by the death of Christ; at the altar he learns again, in the power of living example, who he is; Christ identifies him again for himself, not by a mere phrase, but by an interior renewal. He learns here that the apostle will be a redeemer, or he will be nothing at all. Either his solicitude will bring him to death and resurrection by grace, or it will destroy itself in a sterile, bitter regret; because, quite simply, apart from the altar one cannot do enough, one cannot change men, one does not even know the point at which to begin.

The act of Calvary also reminds the apostle of the practical identity between his love for the Church and his love for Christ. There is no separating the one Person Who was born, died and rose again for the sake of the Church, His own Body. The Body of Christ born of Mary, the Body of Christ immolated on the altar, the Body of Christ building Itself through charity in time; here are not separate Realities, but one; existing under different modes, but still, in Augustine's phrase, "one Christ loving himself." And in Olier's intention: "Our Lord's aim in multiplying His body" is to make "but one Church of all the world, of all men but one worshipper; of all their voices, but one praise; of all their hearts, but one victim in Himself." If one were to reduce the unequivocal phrase of St. Paul, "You are the Body of Christ," to a mere comparison, to the moral person of communal religious sentiment, to a union of minds or action or common purpose undertaken by the community—this would be to misread the definition of the Church given us by Revelation, to "exteriorize" grace out of existence. The Church, according to St. Paul, according to Christ's words in St. John, according to the sacramental notion of the Eucharist, of marriage, of baptism—is the extension of the Word Incarnate in time, the presence of the Risen Savior among men, achieving itself in charity, manifest in communal worship and service; a true supernatural organism, with its own members, services, "positions." This is the work of one and the same Spirit, Who distributes His gifts as He will to each severally.

To the elaboration of this unity in Christ underlying a human variety, Paul devotes the whole of Chapter 12 of the First Letter to the Corinthians; and his conclusion is as lucid as the formula of Eucharistic consecration itself. Paul concludes, "And you are Christ's Body, organs of it depending on one another."

Love for the Mystical Body, the will to suffer for the men in the Church, love for the Person of the Savior: three facets of a single apostolic love. By them the apostle's love is saved from the idolatry of the past and given a vitally present object; he is transformed into a co-worker with the Redeemer, in the same sense as the early apostles were, when they accompanied the Lord in His ministry, witnessed His resurrection, and consecrated His Body at the altar. Like John, the apostle of today recognizes in the Church "that Word Who is life, what He was from the first, what we have heard about Him, what our own eyes have seen of Him; what it was that met our gaze and the touch of our hands." Suffering for the sake of the Church, the apostle suffers for the "completion of Him Who is in every place complete." He "fills up in his own body what is wanting to the sufferings of Christ"; wanting, that is, not because His life and death were insufficient to save the world, but "wanting" in a gracious act of Divine courtesy: Christ's will to join to His death all the sufferings of men for the sake of the continuing Redemption.

The apostle's solicitous love is Catholic, then, not only in a geographical sense spoken of earlier; he is Catholic in time. He is the most far-reaching of men, the man granted a longer life on earth than even Methuselah, because his love of Christ, like a living heart, dilates to include the whole of his race, from the first who walked the earth, to the death of the last son of man. And this is no mere wrench of the imagination, no violent effort to be what one is not; the out-stretched arms of Christ on Calvary, that great gesture which is re-newed every morning through His priesthood, does not merely embrace the men of one or another period of history, but "gathers into a unity all the children of God who are scattered abroad." The man of the Church meditates those texts in which our Lord expressed His longing to unite all men in the one fold, under the one Shep-herd; one as He and the Father are one; and he sees in them some-thing infinitely more than the expansion of a great human heart; they are the absolute will of a Divine Person, expressed in lowly human terms. "Come to me all you who labor and are heavily burdened, and I will refresh you." This is not the cry of a human healer; it is the command of God. "On that day he cried out with a loud voice, saying, 'If any man thirst, let him come to Me and drink. . . .' Whereupon Jesus cried aloud in the temple, 'You know Me, and you know whence I come.' . . . I am the light of the world. He who follows Me can never walk in darkness; he will possess the light which is life." These texts are a human work, a human invitation, indicat-ing tenderness, compassion, with a poignant undercurrent of sorrow for the meager response of men; but they are also a Divine com-mand; they appoint human life to a unique direction; a form that men must take if they are ever to achieve their destiny.

So the solicitude of the apostle does not lead him into a void, does not drain his life's energies, or waste his devotion on a lost cause. This Christ is the Lord of glory. The apostle is at the service of One Who wills absolutely to be served. All the invitations of Christ to men are finally distilled in the command to the apostles: "All authority in heaven and on earth is given to Me; you therefore must go out making disciples of all nations, and baptizing them in the name of the Father and of the Son and of the Holy Ghost, teaching them to observe all the commandments which I have given you. And behold, I am with you all through the days that are coming, until the consummation of the world."

It is this supreme sentence, filled with a Divine assurance, that gives the suffering, the solicitude of the apostle its guarantee. He is not trying to vivify an example that had validity once, but is now dependent on the individual genius or enterprise of those who perpetuate it. He is the witness of the living God in the world He made and died for. He preaches a death which was the passage to victory. He is the instrument of an interior creation without which man will forever be a stranger to himself and the world he walks.

For the apostle is promised victory by the same Christ Who is its substance. In this profound sense he already possesses his victory; Christ is his Life. "He who eats my flesh and drinks my blood, lives continually in me, and I in him . . . if anyone eats of this bread, he shall live forever." All this is obvious, and is often adverted to. But there is another guarantee of victory, achieved literally through the flesh of the neighbor, who is "the Body of Christ." "I was hungry, and you gave me to eat; thirsty, and you gave me to drink. . . . Believe me, when you did it to one of the least of my brethren here, you did it to me." The bond between these two texts has for its strength the very promise of Christ. The man who receives the Body of the Savior as a principle of life, who labors because of It, for Its sake, who accepts the consequent suffering as a transformed man of the Redemption, he it is who wins the victory.

And the Body of Christ is not destined for the altars only; It is for men. Not only the worship offered the Body of Christ that is to be communal, for the call to worship is a call to service. This Body is meant to engraft men, muscle and bone, heart's blood and labor, on one another. "You are the Body of Christ, and member for member." By a rigorous logic Paul passes from an exposition of the marvelous harmony and diversity of the Body of Christ, to "show you a way which is better than any other." The way is, at least partially, service to the Body in charity—to "give away all I have, to feed the poor"; . . . to "give myself, to burnt at the stake . . ." The Body of Christ is ordered to build up the Body of Christ. There are not two Christs in the world; there is but one, existing in a Mystical Unity under different mysteries; in the first case He is the active principle of sanctification; in the second He is the Mystery Who wills more and more to be manifested in the souls of men, in view of a total victory which the last day will witness.

At the center of the Mystery of Christ, sacramental and mystical, stands the apostle, sanctifier and sanctified; it is he who receives (or, in the case of the priesthood, immolates) the Body of Christ for the sake of that same Body which lives by His grace. The apostle does not leave the altar to enter the world; he merely turns from one epiphany of Christ to another. But only if he will "follow through" with the great Sacrament: only if he will realize and admit to heart, through the working of the Sacrament in his soul, the Presence that awaits his labor and love. He must know that Christ is not only "true God of true God, Son substantial with the Father," but "the First-born of every creature"; that the Father "has made him the Head to which the whole Church is joined, so that the Church is His body. . . ." It is true for the Church of all times as it was for the Ephesians that "in Him it was our lot to be called, singled out beforehand to suit His purpose . . . we were to manifest His glory."

One labors and suffers for the sake of the Church because one loves her, the great showing forth of the charity of the Father in His Son. One suffers in the Church because, in a supreme choice of God's love one has been summoned by God, singled out, to continue the paschal mystery in time; to attain glory, but through a death. To suffer for the Church. The apostle will find that this is no easy love, filled with privileges and leisure. Such a love on any plane would be its own condemnation; it shames itself by coming forward. For every love worthy of the name achieves itself by a death; love goes toward greater love by this narrow door.

The Redeemer took up His cross; He demanded the same of those who would profess His name. He declared that the seed that looked toward a harvest must be buried; it must die, or itself remain alone. On the plane of history, the theme is constant; there has never been an apostle in the Church whose life has not undergone the death of Jesus. Perfection of personality, human achievement, power over others, repute among men; all the fruits of a religion that risks being centered on self—these are the "things of a child" which the maturity of grace puts away or learns to do without. From the moment when he has first answered the call of the apostolate, a man is often enough lost; lost to reputation, lost to comforts and compensations, lost to the perfecting of his natural gifts; love of reading, music, art, time and opportunity to fulfill his natural gifts. Père Voillaume writes in this vein to the Little Brothers of Jesus:

What significance would there be in your having a well-regulated existence, a carefully-worked-out schedule and minds at rest, if it were to keep you from being wrenched away from your egoism and handed over, bound hand and foot, as it were, to a love which must take possession of everything in you, leaving you without the slightest corner of yourself to take refuge in? The love toward which Jesus is leading you, led Him to his death on the cross. . . . Your lives are going to be difficult lives, hard lives, jostled and comfortless lives, but God does not wish you to be sheltered. Our vocation is to go out to meet love, by this other road.

And through all the process, the man who suffers in the Church is content to be hidden there. The grain of wheat achieves its identity by being buried; out of sight, out of mind. The God who sees in secret, rewards in secret. Nothing outré, nothing singular, no attempt to draw attention; the apostle's life is quietly ordered in the midst of the brethren, indistinguishable from theirs, finding its validity in hidden service rather than in judgment. For all that meets the eye, he is simply another in the company; no striking of attitudes, no self-justification, but a quiet urbanity of manner, self-possession without pride, labor without complaint, the instinctive choice of what is hidden and of service: "I am in the midst of you as one who serves."

Indeed, his whole idea of suffering in the Church is subordinated to a master attitude, the ideal of uncalculating service. He may wish in his heart that his life would count for something in the scales of world salvation; to have had an effect in the health of the Body; not to thin out or dissipate the riches of Christ as they reach him and are circulated through him to others. This is all to the good, a noble selflessness; but it is God, he realizes, Who makes the final judgment on the effectiveness of a lifetime; he is content with that; and in the meantime, would take it as a betrayal that he should consider himself superior. It is not only his body that he bends to service; it is his will; his is that mind "which was in Christ Jesus."

And this call to suffering and to eventual glory he reads in the text of the sacraments, as they continually touch upon his life, and draw him to glory. To glory: but with what human and lowly means?

He understands that he has been baptized into a death; that in baptism "the old man has been crucified in Christ Jesus." The death of Christ has cast its shadow over his life; he is dead now with that dolorous death by which Christ destroyed the rule of sin in men. A vocation to suffering therefore in his; no one who has reached an interior knowledge of himself will dream that the struggle with sin is canceled. No: but the death of baptism is the type of a daily death which the apostle continues to inflict on himself; death to egoism, to the living of "his own life" apart from usefulness to all. Now his life is to be in conformity with the grace first conferred in the sacrament, and announcing, in the structure of the seed, the whole achievement of mature holiness.

But the death of baptism was a simultaneous birth, a birth into the glory of the Risen Christ. It is remarkable how St. Paul refuses to separate the death and rising of the Savior, both in their historic meaning and in their application to the soul of the Christian. To speak of Catholicity as a religion of death, or of the destiny of the soul as death, is to reduce the Faith to the level of a pessimistic pagan ritual; the will toward extinction as an escape from an intolerable present. But the Savior spoke of His death tranquilly and in an eternal repose of heart within the Father's Plan, on the night before He died: "a passage to the Father." And it is so for the man who believes. Suffering is an ingredient of glory; it is marked on the laborious, stigmatized body of the Church; but only for a time, only as long as time lasts. Until the last day, this countenance is one of labor and humiliation, of neglect and persecution; the nations have not known "the gift of God"; but the features, which are those of Christ's own, will receive the reward of His glorified Body.

To this theme the Apostle devotes some of the most glorious words ever to fall from man's lips: words which had their intensely practical and immediate consequence of impelling Paul forward to "redeem the time," to announce the hour, while salvation was still at hand. "Christ is the first-fruits, and after Him follow those who belong to Him, those who have put their trust in His return. . . ." The light of the resurrection falls upon the darkest hours of man, filling him with a virile comfort, an unbreakable courage. "For ourselves, we are being hampered everywhere, yet still have room to breathe, are hard put to it, but never at a loss; persecution does not leave us unbefriended, nor crushing blows destroy us; we carry about continually in our bodies the dying state of Jesus; so that the living power of Jesus may be manifested in our bodies too."

How heartening it is, this voice that reaches across time and death, to remind men: baptism is the living pattern of action, the matrix of Christian attitudes, that form from which man faces his world, and achieves its conquest, which is Christ's own! To act otherwise, to fall disheartened from the task, to excuse the hardships of life out of life, to seek for substitutes for the hard present task, to ignore the call to labor and community effort, friendship, sacrifice of time and self-will; all this is to demand the reward of eternity without paying the price. But the voice of Paul is an utterly uncompromising yes of the apostolic heart; intense, laborious, unwearying: "We do not play the coward; though the outward part of our nature is being worn down, our inner life is refreshed from day to day. This light and momentary affliction brings with it a reward multiplied every way, loading us with everlasting glory; if only we will fix our eyes on what is unseen, not on what we can see. . . ."

VIII
Prayer

The Word Incarnate was a Man of prayer. This statement, to which
the Gospel bears witness, must be taken as part of the scandal of the
Incarnation. The eternal God in a human body turns in acknowl-
edgment toward the Father at every great moment of His life; a
prayer intensely and completely human, marked by anguish, a
shrinking from suffering, a cry for strength; a prayer that is most
poignant and winning as He faced the spectacle of death. And
through every event one recognizes the living unity which the Father
declared in Him, and which declared the Father to men. Prayer was
not one ingredient in the Life of Christ, in the sense that it could
easily have been dispensed with, and the truth of the Incarnation
suffer no diminution. Prayer, like suffering, like love of men, like
the necessity of giving Himself, was a mark of this human nature,
united to this Divine Person; now able to express for the first time,
in a human body, the Divine Act from eternity; able to express how
God would act, if He were man.

So: if God were man, He would suffer for men, because His
human Heart expressed not only an immense and pure and inclusive
human love for all other men; but because, at the same time, this
Heart was the organ, the expression, the corporal and visible reality
of a love which had been hidden from eternity in the Word of the

Father. And this will to suffer would not arise primarily out of any decree, conceived as extrinsic to the Act of God; but God, being supreme freedom, acted (suffered) in this way; because in this way a vivid, dimensional, and permanent proof of the eternal love for men would be offered men.

So, too, if God were man, He would be a man of prayer. The prayer of the Word Incarnate is a lovely and inseparable footnote to the text: The Word was made flesh. For the text to be complete, for its resonance to reach man's heart intact and true, it was necessary that He be a Man of prayer; and this, not as a historical ideal now discoverable only in a text of scripture; but that He might be, today and forever, the very Form and Substance of approach to the Father; the One Who is eternally at the door, at man's side; the One Whose promises in regard to prayer stand firm, because He is their Divine guarantee; the One Who finally, in the Holy Sacrifice, sweeps all the words from man's lips and hearts, and speaks to the Father in his place, through the renewal of the one Act that finally makes all prayer His own.

As far as an eyewitness could have discerned, the prayer of Christ was a determined act of turning toward, of remaining present to, the Father, with all the energies of His human mind and heart. Of course, in reality, the prayer of the Word Incarnate brings an infinitely richer scene, a mystery. It is the visible expression of that Presence of Son to Father which defines eternity. "I am in the Father; the Father is in Me." Knowledge and love, mutual penetration, is all Their gift. "All Thy possessions are mine." So all the life of the three Persons of the Trinity is a prayer; if one understands the act of love, total knowledge of another, sharing of gifts.

But it was the Word in a human body Who, in the days of His flesh, prayed "with a strong cry and tears, and was heard for His reverence." Here with the prayer of Equal to Equal, the eternal and immutable act of love and knowledge of Father and Son, is also the approach of the Man to God—a Man of labors, Master of apostles, Teacher of men, Man of sorrows, Priest on the eve of His sacrifice; all these moments marked that urgent confronting of the Father with this perfect humanity. His Son the Man.

This prayer is supremely free. It is not in bonds to a sense of guilt, to a need of redemption, to the fact of hell, to the necessity of struggle toward personal salvation; all that is best and most divine in man was here, in humanity's Firstborn. Whatever mars or troubles man's prayer, from the effects of personal or original sin, was absent from this prayer. If there was hope present in it, His trust was the strong and joyous trust that His sacred body would attain Its glory, and the meeting ground between Christ and men; in hope, the Son of God joins them to His prayer. He hopes for men because He loves them. Adoration, thanksgiving, supplication; He moves among the infinite goods of His Father, and dispenses them with the freedom of a Son. "Whatever you ask the Father in my name, He will grant it to you." And then turning to the Father, "Father, I pray that they may be one, as You and I are one," or again, "that where I am, these may also be." And on another occasion, turning to His own with a divine assurance, "Whatever you ask the Father in my name, that He will grant you. . . ."

So his prayer, in so many of its facets, on so many occasions, is a subtle interplay of the Divine with the human; a reminder, delicate and sure, of the way the Divine embraces the human, is intent upon it, changes it, works with it, constantly is at pains that it realize its own possibility for expansion and glory. "Through Christ our Lord," "I am the door." To the Divine, through this Body, the passage is plain for men. He has prayed for them. This is not only an immediate conclusion of His priesthood; He was at pains to make the fact even more explicit; to Peter, before his fall, and during the Last Supper, to the community of apostles.

Prayed for what? Most of all that His own Sonship be extended through all mankind. As He is the gift of the Father, the Substance of the Father, the sum of all the Father will have to say of Himself, so He prays that the gift of Sonship may be granted men "that the love Thou hast bestowed on Me may dwell in them, and I too may dwell in them. . . ." This is the keystone of Christ's prayer for men. Realizing by nature what it is to be Son of the Father; at the other pole, loving man with God's own love; being in Himself the total love of the Father; realizing to the heart what it is to be man; knowing man's need to find himself by abandoning himself, knowing in His infinite completeness man's wounds and fissures; being finally so qualified to define man's sickness and to diagnose it, to know man's need and to fulfill it, His prayer ascends to the Father, with a Son's boldness, and asks of Him that gift that will raise whole generations of sons to His image. "That they may have life, and have it more abundantly."

This prayer of Christ for men is divinely serious; it refuses to linger on the periphery of man's life, to ask for what is merely provisional in the face of essential need, to grant a gift that in any way will stop short of eternity. Christ had certainly ratified prayer for temporal benefits; He had instructed the twelve to pray for daily bread; but when the hour struck for the High Priest to pray for His people, the solemn hour before His death, it was an astonishing request that rose from His heart and lips; the temporal could be dispensed with or postponed, or presupposed; this was simply not the time; what He asked then was a union with Himself which would make all men sons of the same Father: "That they may be one, as Thou, Father, and I are one . . . that while Thou art in me, I may be in them, so they may be perfectly made one."

This is the prayer for mankind by the one Man Who was quite literally God. Because it was the prayer of God, it has been answered. This is not a favor which it was left to men to ask, or whose answer remains in doubt. The one Spirit Who formulated the prayer also guaranteed, in innumerable places, its fulfillment; in the prophets and their words of union under the figure of bride and bridegroom, in St. Paul's sentences on the Mystical Body and its Head, one in effort, love, and destiny; in Christ's own words, on the occasion of his prayer: "I am the vine, you are the branches": that is, what was a request made of the Father was simultaneously a gift from the Father; a fact, fulfilled.

His prayer for men has created them again to His image. Where there had been dissention, scattering, illusion, hopelessness, all the interior anarchy that followed on sin, ignorance of one's destiny now and hereafter—now there are unity, common effort and love, intelligence, sacrifice, and growth. The prayer of God, followed by the death of God, has done this. Such is the peak of the Divine commerce among men; from now forward it is inaccurate to speak of Him and mankind as two realities—and so speaking or thinking, to suppose one had reached either reality; this Man forms with men a single supernatural entity. "We too, all of us, have been baptized into a single Body, all of us. . . . And you are Christ's Body. . . . We are limbs of His Body; flesh and bone, we belong to Him. . . ."

The great fact consequent on the prayer of Christ, and its being granted, is this: every prayer now belongs to the Church in an absolute sense. It proceeds from the grace she mediates, because the formula "all grace through Christ" implies all grace through the Church; which is not a reality other than He, but Himself. Every prayer leads in the direction of the Church; from the first glimmerings of faith to the last grace of perseverance, the prayer of men is answered so that they may have her life, and share it more abundantly. No prayer could be anything but an illusion, and not lead men toward her; since she is in Christ, and Christ is in the Father, to Whose face men are destined.

So certain consequences follow; prayer cannot be private in any negative sense. No prayer can ask for its own way to the Father; what it asks is at once a personal and social grace; that the life of the vine be more abundantly shared by the branches, that one be joined more securely, buried more deeply, in the Church; that as living members, efficiency, flexibility, usefulness, a deep sense of serving the whole Body may be activated more and more.

In becoming more and more a man of prayer in the Church, a man is transformed in two ways; his social sense is intensified, and his character is more strongly individuated. Before the face of Christ, he is progressively set apart as unique, an absolute, a being that defies imitation. It was in this way that a German mystic was reminded of grace when she walked abroad on a cold morning, and saw the meanest weeds transformed by the frost that lay upon them; all the structure of leaf and stem wonderfully glorified and individualized; and her first thought was of grace, and its gift of fineness, uniqueness; its hatred of mediocrity and sameness.

But prayer in the Church is not meant to set up a class of initiates or esoterics; from the point of view of being, it makes the soul more and more a soul; and effectively it puts the soul to work. Communal prayer refuses man the luxury of a private perfection; it casts his destiny out on the deep. It gives man a larger stake in the eternity of all men, especially of all who are at this moment working out their salvation in and by the Church. The grave, challenging voice of the Church reaches him; no one can be saved alone; everyone is brother of his brother, flesh of his flesh. There is one common voice to all men; in some cases muffled, incoherent, unconscious of its own need for help; but addressed, whether it know or not, to the common Father of all. It is for the man of the Church to direct and refine the cacophonies of this voice; to speak for it where necessary, to modulate it, to interpret, to remind the Father what it is striving so desperately and pitifully to say.

For the Catholic is, by baptism, Christ to all men. He stands in the relation of son to the Eternal Father, and when he prays it is the pleading adoration of His own Son that the Father hears: "that they may be one, as Thou, Father, in me, and I in Thee."

It would seem to be a law of grace that the man praying in and with the Church finds his moorings slipped, and himself cast off into the redemptive adventure of Christ. "Follow Me." He discovers the Father more readily, more naturally at prayer; as the one Lodestone of life; and in discovering the Father his vocation to men deepens unutterably. He moves forward conscious of representing all men: those moving in the Father's direction; those without hope, those in danger of destruction; the whole dolorous procession of humanity.

Do men dream of really doing something, of changing things in the world? No apostle but is tempted now and then by a subtle and terrible temptation of failure; the quantitative failure of the Church to win the whole world to itself. Numbers are on the increase; but the heart sinks to realize that a weight of evil suffocates so many labors, that the Church is fishing with a fragile line in a sea teeming with life. The laborers are few. They are few in numbers, few in daring, few in enthusiasm, few in vision. Chances slip by, time is lost, men are left in the questionable position they were born into; there are so few miracles, so few miraculous men; when work should move along quickly to term, with the illumination and strength of grace, it is hobbled by a tradition hardened into routine, by an apostolic spirit sunken into clericalism. Each one has his private sorrows, which are public in effect; because they witness faults which reduce the full impact of Christ's grace.

The only thing that will save, that will literally save reason, peace, effectiveness, is a deliberate death, an entrance into faith, the willingness to die in a mystery. The apostle in the Church not as judge, but as man of prayer; judgment of the world is not delegated to him; its salvation is. The plunge into the prayer of the Church, like the plunge into its baptism, is a death to human discernment, to human reaction; it is a death, but simultaneously a resurrection; the entrance into a new world. And as this world is one of faith, its landscape is darkened, the truth in a faulty mirror, hidden to the senses and to merely human judgment.

And what does one learn about the Church, in this new existence of prayer, whose passport is CREDO? That though the signs of defeat surround human life, the Church already wears a countenance of victory: "I have overcome the world. . . . Do not be afraid; I am before all; I am the end of all, and I live: I who underwent death, am alive, as thou seest, to endless ages, and I hold the keys of death and hell. . . . Keep faith with Me to the point of death, and I will crown thee with life. . . ." Men need a taste of victory; faith assures them; the victory has been won. What is left is its dolorous reaping, for the sake of the generation now living. But men will never be messengers of victory, or taste a victory whose ingredient is temporal defeat, without experiencing that cycle which was the Savior's, and which is His process of love for those who follow. Victory is His final word for His creation; it sums up the cross in the resurrection. It sums up history, which goes the same sorrowful way as its Master. But the victory is mysterious, for the present; it is achieved in souls, not in bodies. It can only be apprehended by an interior gaze that is impatient of appearances, that wills to encounter Christ in the defeat of the cross; so to be healed, and to become a healer. On the contrary, men who do not pray are lost; lost first of all in the appearances of things, which are a lie. They are a lie, not because they pretend to exist (they do in fact exist), but because they presume to be all of reality, or even its major part. But faith reminds; what one sees or touches or hears, what one experiences as defeat, is only the infinitesimal part of things as they are.

And what defines "things as they are"? What is the truest face of reality? Every man is plunged into the death of the Savior, is destined for His face, is born and lives and dies within the compass of an unwearying, magnificent love. Of the ways in which this love encompasses its will, men know very little; and even that little he knows, how circumscribed are his judgments, how ridiculous and paltry are the limits he would set to the energy and ingenuity of divine love!

In and with the Church at prayer, these things come home to the secret places of the soul; what it is to be a creature, and not to preempt, even under pretense of the apostolate, the Providence of God. What grows in the soul of the man at prayer in the Church is a sane and holy balance of attitudes which are the Church's own. Serenity and fullness of labor: redeeming the time from the perspective of eternity, experiencing the thirst of Christ for souls, an inner, invigorating certainty of victory. A willingness to continue the Passion by undergoing it, a sense of direction in darkness; moving toward the empty tomb.

And as prayer becomes more and more infused with the mind of Christ, it will share not only in His requests, but in His sense of values. In regard to daily bread and the needs of the body, a fine sense of independence, a trust in the Father, Who clothes the lilies of the fields, and is provident to the birds of the air. In regard to suffering, the prayer of the man of the Church will always be modified, as was that of Christ: Not my will, but Thine be done. It is good that the human will declare its anguish; it is also good that it yield before the will of God. In so doing, it is not destroyed, but purified, and made fit to become an instrument of redemption in the hands of the God of love.

But in proportion as one's prayer is joined in spirit to the prayer of Christ, it will share in the absolute assurance of being heard. There is finally one prayer from which the Father cannot turn: that His Son be glorified in His Mystical Body. Is one's prayer then of adoration, or thanksgiving, of request, of sorrow for sin, or that simple resting in the presence of God which really includes all these, because the whole person is present to Him? It makes no difference; all who pray, all who beg personal favors whose import affects the

person painfully and truly, all who persevere at prayer in spite of
mood and state of health and mind—all are saying the same thing:
"Glory to God in the highest . . . That they may be one, as Thou,
Father, in me, and I in Thee . . . Glory be to the Father and to the
Son and to the Holy Spirit . . . Holy, Holy, Holy . . . Give us this
day our daily bread . . ." The soul who prays in his baptism prays
in Christ; he is a member of Christ, praying with the words of his
Master, with his Master's heart. He is heard.

Such prayer deserves the name "liturgical"; it continues the
prayer of Christ, in and through His Church. Joined to the prayer
of the Mediator, it continues with a divine seriousness the request
of His last hour: for unity among men, for union with the Father.
And as the prayer of the whole Christ, it grants the people of God,
as they turn to the Father, a form, a voice that deserves to win His
approval: the beloved son of His good pleasure. And such prayer,
ordered, conscious of human limitation and growth, is the prayer
of the Church: mindful of God, mindful of men.

It would be easy to conceive of a prayer of supermen, or of
pure spirits, that would move, along a single plane of light and on
an undeviating line, toward God. Such a prayer would be untrou-
bled by emotional states, in need of no rhythm of mood or alterna-
tion of energy, expressing itself unchangeably in an adoration that
said everything. No events would mar its surface or break its intensity into high or low points. Sorrow would not darken its spectrum,
nor joy brighten it suddenly. Such is the prayer of the angels:
". . . without end saying, Holy, Holy, Holy." But the prayer of the
Church of Christ is otherwise. Humanity has a history, sacred and
profane; its progress across the page of the world is marked by nobility and horror, by great moments and moments of degradation;
marked most of all, by the "deeds of God," by the repeated insistence
of God that He be not kept at a distance from the work of His
hands, that He be not locked out of the world He created. And
finally, the "Mystery" is summed up in the supreme Gift: "the Word
is made flesh, and dwelt among us." A Gift has arrived; the eternally
Other is now present.

And the Gift of Christ was not merely lent to men for a few
years of time; what was once assumed was never abandoned; the

risen Christ is released into the universe of men—His mandate from the Father, His power over human ills, His prayer. What is true of the physical Christ is true of His mystical life in the Church. "I am with you all days." In the life of the Savior among men, a certain order of events was observable; a birth, a hidden life, a public life, a death, a resurrection and ascension to the Father. And as events in time must be, these followed one upon the other; not in random order, but in a manifestly human one. The Word Incarnate was a subject of time; He asked no concessions from time; but before He was a man, He was a child; and before that an infant; and before that, a burden in His mother's body. Before He died in our midst, He underwent the humiliating process which alone can bring on the stage of the world a mature man.

Now it is these events of Emmanuel which the liturgy strives to bring before men, in the order in which they occurred, according to their original cycle, their energies, released into the invisible order of grace, now at the disposal of all believers. Their supreme value is to make present and available to man the life which saved man once for all, but whose saving power still awaits the event of man's welcome.

A period of preparation, first of all. Man must repeat and make his own those purifying sentiments of hope and penance which were the vocation of Israel as it awaited its Savior. Bethlehem is viewed from afar; the Messiah is discerned first dimly, then with growing clarity on the horizon of time. In a state of self-imposed stillness and longing, man learns his own insufficiency; and learns to cry, with the voice of all humanity, "Come and save us." By the absence of the Gift he learns Its supreme value, so that Its eventual presence will never be taken for granted. And this state of soul is no unrealistic play-acting; it is still true to say of mankind, and of each soul, that it is perpetual Advent; that it represents an unfinished triumph of God. In order to deserve his further gifts, man must experience his own creaturehood and learn by a practiced humility to shun pride which would reject the Savior when He appears quietly in his gift of grace. "There has stood in your midst One Whom you do not know."

Then, a period of infancy and childhood. The Savior is present

in His world, but the only sign of Presence is the shattering humiliation of the child at Mary's knee. Before the activity of the Gospel
will draw Him among men, He learns to the heart the meaning of
time; He learns to take time seriously by undergoing its process, by
experiencing the world He created, by groping for its sounds and
colors; a possession of creation which spells the laborious effort
toward maturity. And in the same period, lived again in the liturgy
of the Christmas cycle, man enters once more into spiritual childhood; to learn patience; and the gracious ways of grace, that do not
force growth, or wring time from its own uses; but are patient and
deals with time on its own terms. "He was subject to them. . . . He
advanced in wisdom and age and grace. . . ." The infancy of the
Savior is an affront to superman. He cannot understand that grace
comes "as dew upon the fleece"; gently and gradually restoring, fulfilling, completing, healing. And in view of the active life of the
apostle, the hidden life warns him; greatness before God is not the
announcement of headlines or the great names of this world; it
lives out of the sight of men. Its presence is radically a mystery; the
elevated presence of those who suffer and labor in secret, content that
the heavenly Father sees and rewards. This cycle of the liturgy speaks
to the sick and the old, to those who will make no stir in the world
by reason of talent or force of personality, but who possess the one
essential—the secret of grace as it faces the world and seeks to save
it; a mysterious life transmitted out of sight and hearing, from generation to generation, enabling man to live the hidden life and so to
save others. To those who will never leave Nazareth, the lowly house
of personal deficiency, of the one talent—"He went down with
them . . . and was subject to them"—the liturgy of the hidden life
comes as a guarantee; Christ was no less Savior of men when He
dwelt in this mysterious apartness, while the imperial nation made
its momentary stir, and history passed Him by.

Some will know a public life, constant and demanding, until
death. To them the liturgy says: you must dig roots deep into the
substratum of grace, or you condemn your words to the periphery of
life, your actions to superficiality. Unless one has submitted himself
to the discipline of silence and obscurity, and learned to possess his
own soul, the voice of nature will later preempt his message; he will

preach only himself, or a temporal salvation, or any one of the subtle extremes of nature which borrow the phrases of the Gospel after having emptied it of its substance. So in full manhood, the Word Incarnate takes the center of the local stage, gathers His men about Him, and the work of the Kingdom is manifest among men. The flower nurtured in the darkness of Nazareth springs into the light of human day. "The Word . . . dwelt among us. . . ." "And we saw His glory, as of the only-begotten of the Father, full of grace and truth. . . ." The content of that substantial Mystery, a Person, hidden from the foundations of the world, is revealed in the Son: "Behold, I come." And the work of grace is a social enterprise; the Word of God goes forth, disturbing the atmosphere of time, reaching, in succession, the twelve, the seventy-two, the crowds; and finally, through the Divine Mandate, slips the bonds of all time and place: "Go into the whole world. . . . I am with you all days, even to the consummation of the world." And the outward circles of that "grace and truth" reach man again through the public cycle of the liturgy. What does he learn as he ponders the texts of the Gospels and the Acts of the Apostles? The divinely human synthesis of the Church; its dolorous beginnings, its setbacks at the hands of the powers of this world, of betrayals in its midst; the gigantic stature of heart required of the apostle; discernment, courage, staying power; independence of the Kingdom from temptation to power and establishment. . . . Before the inner eye of the worshiper is spread the vast panorama of the Church in history, from the tentative local beginnings of the Acts, through the larger Mediterranean world of Paul and his companions; those first and wonderful days when the blood of Christ was still warm on the altars, and His memory green among men. . . . And all for what? So that reading aright these texts, the apostle today may come to sense the underlying harmony of the apostolic attitude; with what mind he must go forward, what he must learn to expect of himself and others, without being scandalized or defeated: so that in the midst of crushing labor and the demands of men, he may keep to his true center, the inner integrity of grace that alone will save his apostolate from falling away to another merely human undertaking. Straight at his heart are aimed the burning sentences of Paul, words which are no desiccated for-

mulae, but quick with the blood that had been offered again and
again to the Father: "in labors, in watchings, in persecution"; "for
the sake of His Body, the Church."

The apostle, finally, must see his activity as the continuation of
a mystery which had its deepest expression on Calvary. Paul the
Apostle speaks: "I bear about in my body the wounds of the Lord
Jesus." And the wounds are not only a personal possession; through
the body of the apostle, through his free act of immolation, the
wounds of Christ are impressed on the members of Christ's Mystical
Body; His sufferings overflow; the apostolate will be authentic if it
bears the wounds of the Master into the world, that the total Christ
may face the Father with the living evidence of love upon it.

So the liturgy insists upon the living unity of the public life with
the passion. "I die daily" is the tranquil Pauline summary of his
labors. Death to selfishness, death to convenience, death to one's
own disposal of time and energy, death to a quiet minimum of work
or a privileged atmosphere of honor and inner repose; death to
equilibrium of human prudence presuming to dictate what one can
do, what must be left undone. And upon the stage of life enter difficulty, danger, uprooting, human interference, blindness; in sum,
the Passion of Christ as the life of one's life: "Always bearing about
in our bodies the death of Jesus, that the life of Jesus may be seen
in us." "And so they crucified Him there." The labor of the apostle
is crowned, is made acceptable, by his death. He is finally a giver of
life because he freely gives his own life, time and again in the midst
of his labor; now definitively, by passage to the Father. Death is the
proving ground of the apostle; it elevates his labors to the dignity of
redemption. All the repeated deaths to which he had submitted are
a preparation for this moment, in which his being is not simply
wrenched apart like that of an animal; but in vindicated freedom he
speaks once for all a death which is salvific: "No man takes my life
from me, but I lay down my life freely." To die in Christ Jesus is to
die as priest and redeemer, in the supreme act of self-immolation that
will sum up a lifetime, a continual death for the sake of the flock.

This is what the liturgy of passiontide reminds the apostle; that
as his public life has been conformed to the ministry of Christ, so
now his death. The apostle has become a redeemer, in this plenary

act, undergone in the image of the death that first saved us; a free, human, reasonable decision, an obedience aware of all implications; the willingness to enter a door so strait and narrow that one's very body must be left behind.

But this very death, continues the voice of the liturgy, is an entrance into glory. The period of the resurrection brings an atmosphere of victory; a victory which is the atmosphere of the apostolate itself; since the labors of the active life are bathed in the presence of the Risen Christ. "I have risen, and I am still with you." He is with us, says the liturgy, not as a matter of unfounded hope or surface optimism; but the Risen Christ is reproducing in men the very form of His resurrection through the Eucharist, His Body in glory; through the sacraments, which are the ineffable "drawing" of men in the direction of eternity.

IX

The Sacrifice

It is interesting to reflect on how a human action, once accomplished, often manages to live on in time, and even to achieve a kind of immortality. The Dutch woman of the sixteenth century, busied with preparing a meal in the cold morning light of a country inn, gave little thought to what she was about, and none at all to the man observing her from a corner table; but her action, trivial and soon forgotten, lives in the glowing canvas of Rembrandt. She has achieved a kind of domestic monumentality, warm and sympathetic, because of the reflective eye that fell on her actions and enlarged them; still recognizable under the corrosive hand of time, she and her duties rise to meet every human morning, and find their place securely in the changing landscape of history. Her action lives by an artistic representation.

Again, a human action lives, strongly reasserting itself, in the genre of effect. All men are living witnesses to the enduring causality of human love; they represent a prolongation of the love of parenthood, which incarnated itself in them. This love was no mere speculative dream, but a warmly human and passionate state, longing to express itself, to make itself permanent and creative; and it found a way to do all this, through the act of love. The parent regards his child, through all his life, and reads in the young eyes the text of human love, and what it can work: a true creation, an effect that would live on, in a very true sense brushing time aside and preserving, in spite of all defacements, the accurate image of conjugal love; so unselfish, so total; even in a natural sense, so enduring. Their act of love lives on in the child.

It is a truism, again, that the great action of history lives because men imitate it. It has a tenacity, a hold on time that gives it a footing in the high and low tides of human affairs. This is the kind of immortality Cicero dreamed of: the corner that men would turn because of the map he had traced for them; the direction given the mind of youth by a thought that refused to grow old, but went on and on, propagating itself, pollenizing the atmosphere until all winds bore the seed headlong into the unlikeliest places. Caesar to Napoleon, Cicero to Newman, Sophocles to Shakespeare: the great act, the great thought, lives on by a natural dissemination; it seeks only new soil for a new beginning. And the saints are surely a case in point: Ignatius says expressly that he was embarked on a new road by reading holy lives, and by the query: why could he not do what the saints had done? The Curé D'Ars confessed his heart's blood kindled by the stubborn heartbeat of Regis, so recently dead. And who is to measure with any degree of accuracy what the lives of saints are doing on behalf of the Mystical Body today? Those magnificent, active cells, whose life is not taken away, but only changed for the better, only purified and sublimated by the short passage of death, they are still giving, with a divine freedom, their superabundant life to those who follow, who are still involved in time. Their action lives; by grace, by imitation, by the centrifugal action of love.

Again, an action lives on in time because, in one sense or another, it awaits time to fulfill it. There is a mystery here, of what one can only call a double existence in time. In sacred history, such actions as Moses' crossing of the sea, the guidance of the Jewish people under a cloud, their taking of a certain food and drink in the desert—all these acts had their own historical validity; they truly occurred, at a given date and place. But in the mind of the Holy Spirit they were not finished with. God has a long memory, especially where it is a question of His acting as teacher, of setting out an example, or showing the reach of His love. God was in so many works saying: The gifts I have in mind for you are unheard of; I fear you will undervalue them, not recognize them, not give them the fullness of your attention when they come. So you must undergo a long pedagogy before their coming, a schooling sometimes lasting for thousands of years; so that in the memory of the first gift, the first action, you will take heart and stature to receive the second one, the one I had in mind from the beginning, and receive it as you should. This is Paul's explanation of God's teaching method: "Our fathers . . . all ate the same prophetic rock which bore them company, the rock that was Christ" (I Cor. 10:4), and immediately he adds, "It is we that were foreshadowed in these events. . . ."

And here is the point of all this: one action lived on in time because it was waiting to be given its real meaning, to step out of the shadows of time, minus its disguise. Paul: "When all this happened to them, it was a symbol; the record of it was written as a warning to us, in whom history has reached its fulfillment. . . ." Now, possessing and receiving baptism, the Holy Eucharist, the whole history of the Incarnation, men are in the best position to define what God was doing when He led the disorganized and untrusting Jews across the Red Sea, fed them with manna, gave them Moses for leader. Those first acts, wonderfully as they show God's hand, are mere shadows of what was to come. Their life is a provisory one: they cannot stand alone any more, and the one who reads of them without the long perspective faith can give them misses God's whole point in bringing them about.

There are other ready examples of this kind of conditioned existence, continued in time for the sake of something greater to come. Ruth's fidelity and Judith's courage are read by the Church as an imperfect text of the life of Mary. The great prophets and kings and patriarchs did something wonderfully selfless or holy or wise that made them worthy to remind us of Christ: they are like noble bookmarks inserted in this or that Gospel page by the Holy Spirit; and when men come upon their features, and the message of that page, they discover also the fullest reason for the creation of these men: to place an ineradicable image in the memories of those who followed, so that by piecing together this and that fragment, the countenance of the Redeemer, and the resemblance to Him of all believers of all time, might be discerned. For the men who live after the fulfillment, such lives act as a burning glass, focusing love and attention where they really belong, out of the apparent chaos of history: on the adorable Person of the Word Incarnate and His Church—"For us," says Paul (Hebrews 11:40), "God had something better in store. . . . We were needed, to make the history of their lives complete."

The first call of faith had demanded of Abraham a radical separation from the circumstances of his old life: "Leave thy country behind thee, thy kinfolk, and thy father's home, and come away into a land which I will show thee." The losses his faith will entail are dwelt upon in some exactness; a man must know what he is leaving, and God must be sure he knows, so that the sacrifice of it may be fully human, fully reckoned with. And what is the character of the new land? And what direction leads to it? How will one survive on the way? What arrangements are made for arrival, welcome, new beginnings? No matter. Simply the rigor of the imperative: Come. The way, the how, the term of things, leave to Me; what you need to know is simply this; it is I Who will show it to you; it is I Who will lead you there.

So in one call, the certainty of faith, and its darkness, are vindicated. If the way were manifest, the reward apparent, the details of the journey offered, what would become of the substance of faith? And why should faith "be reckoned of virtue to Abraham"? And the apostle immediately adds: In effect we were present to the act of faith that his great spirit rose to, by grace: his faith was our own; his greatness can never die while, anywhere in time, a man chooses the God Who chooses him. "The words, it was reckoned virtue in him, were not written of him only; they were written of us too. It will be reckoned virtue in us, if we believe in God as having raised our Lord Jesus Christ from the dead. . . ."

A man like Abraham still speaks movingly to the believer because he is the very type of faith. His was the first vocation in sacred history, a vocation that would become the analogue for all who would follow: no faith, of whatever time, would God find pleasing, unless it regarded Him, the world, all reality, from the heights of that choice by which the first man of faith overcame at one blow the evidence of the world, of age, of his own senses, of merely human reasoning; simply, he believed in the promise of God to lead him into a new land and to give him a son; and after that small hope of the race had been safely born against all expectation, to bring a further mighty test to a good outcome.

For Abraham was asked to sacrifice what he loved most; literally and by a death; faith asked the destruction of what faith had erected; the way to God was by a series of deaths. The faith which had seemed total at one period, which had seemed to demand all of one's strength and trust, was rewarded; and then the reward itself was threatened in the fire of an even more rigorous call. "Old as [Sara] was, she conceived and bore a son at the very time God had foretold.". . . "After this, God would put Abraham to the test; so he called to him . . . Take thy only son, thy beloved son Isaac, with thee . . . and offer him to me in burnt-sacrifice on a mountain which I will show thee. . . ."

How cruelly, how compassionately God lingers upon the sweet image of this son! He is the only child, he is the beloved of Abraham's old age; there will be no other. Not only is Isaac desired for his own person, the figure of a lovely boy, come to restore the youth of the old, a light upon the ancient city, a voice in the home long used to silence within and scorn without. Even more: in this youth are summed up, according to the very word of God, all the hopes of Israel. His body is the repository of the promise: "Here is the covenant I make with thee: thou shalt be the father of a multitude of nations. . . . I will make thee fruitful beyond all measure, so that thou shalt count among the nations; from thy issue kings shall rise."

From the slender form of this son, the generations of the chosen race would march; Isaac was the point in which all the future of the nation met; if not through him, then not at all. But faith, in order to be perfect, needs reminding; God is to be preferred above all His gifts, even the most perfect, the most innocent and promising. As He was giver of the gift, and absolute master of human life, He can shatteringly speak His transcendence by demanding the return of the gift.

The demand is of course rescinded, but in the process faith has been marvelously purified. The presence of God, Who is the substance of faith, is sensed more easily by the soul; and the original promise, whose fulfillment was threatened in this crisis of trust, is now mightily reasserted: "I have taken an oath by my own name, to reward thee for this act of thine, when thou wast ready to give up thy only son for my sake; more and more will I bless thee, more and more will I give thee increase to thy posterity, till they are countless as the stars in heaven, or the sand by the seashore. . . ." In Abraham, then, is found the noblest type of that mysterious double existence named by theology "typical." It is not only that he lives on in an eternal life his faith merited for him; but wherever the believer speaks his "Credo" the fatherhood of Abraham is triumphantly reasserted; he is not merely "our forefather by human descent". . . we are "that posterity . . . which imitates his faith." We are "his children in the sight of God, in whom he put his faith. . . ."

So a given action persists in various ways through time; by its representation, by its effects, by a natural imitation, by its fulfillment. Perhaps these reflections will help to illumine the subject of the Mass. The continuance of Calvary in time is certainly not merely "representational," as if a member of the Christian community acted as a kind of mime of Christ, a reverent actor moving props, exciting memory and longing, really accomplishing nothing at all. The idea of a natural imitation also falls short of the reality because it transfers to natural forces of personality and example what is ontologically independent, and makes subject to the high or low point of a collective enthusiasm what God has set apart by a mysterious, inviolate life of its own. Nor can the notion of cause and effect exhaust Calvary living in time: the Mass would be useless if men were automatically to reap the effects of Calvary as a historically unrepeatable act: the Mass, in other words, is not an effect of Calvary; it is Calvary.

In considering the Mass, the believer is in the realm of something unique. No other act of Christ's life is placed entitatively in the Church's hands by a positive command, to be repeated as He once performed it. The Church is given His example to follow through the whole of the Incarnate Mystery, but this is almost infinitely varied, as the saints demonstrate eloquently. On the contrary, in the matter of Calvary living in time, there is to be no least deviation; either the act itself lives, performed by a chosen person, with certain indispensable materials, with a formula that is changeless, with the intention of doing what He did, or it will not be "the death of the Lord" at all. And from a positive view, performed as He willed it, the words once spoken over bread and wine by an ordained priest, Calvary lives, the act of Calvary is accomplished; only the mode of the oblation is different. To come to a formula: the death of the Savior is the only historical action out of all time that lives entitatively in time, that overleaps time with the same features, the same effects, the same divine efficiency. Being what it is, the Mass is a unique and vital conquest of time, a daring act possible only to the Church whose Head, already in eternity, can deal with time as His absolute possession and subject.

There are certain capital consequences for the Church in this act of Calvary re-presented exactly through the Mass and given to her as a possession forever. It was of Calvary she was first of all born; but this birth, accomplished mystically from the opened side of the Savior, is not to be compared univocally with natural birth. The act of being born, humanly speaking, is a separation from the mother. It marks the beginning of an independent life, the point at which an organism has achieved itself as a living entity. The birth of the Church on Calvary, while it brought the Church as an organism into being, certainly had no such disruptive effect as to place her aside ontologically from the Master. She was born of Him that she might remain in Him, of Him forever. All her efficiency still streams from His wounds; from that blood which after two thousand years is still warm on her altars. By the Mass she is reborn continually of Him. Through it, the infinite value of His holy death is concentrated on her throughout all time, preserving the spotless beauty of her first creation. So through the Mass she is forever young. She goes continually to the altar of God; she does not count her age by years, in a growing distance from the date or place of her birth; but she is perennially on Calvary, youthful and strong. Like her Master spoken of in the psalms, she does not grow old. She witnesses the ages of man, and how God changes the centuries like a garment, while she is forever renewed. She has no sad tales in her liturgy to compare with the Greek myth of Tithonus, who asked the gods for unending life, but neglected to ask for youth as well, and so was cursed with a failing old age on the earth: a story which symbolizes perfectly all the strivings for immortality which do not seek it of the Church.

Possessing the renewal of Calvary, the Church can also mediate through all time what our Savior's death accomplished for men. Through Calvary, which is hers alone, she is Jesus to the world. Fed with His blood at its sacred Source, listening eternally to the rhythm and desires of His heart, sharing the divine fecundity of His Spirit, first poured abroad on her at His death, she can assume the words announced by the angel: You will call His name Jesus, because He will save His people from their sins. She possesses the one Victim, Who wills to renew His immolation in an unbloody manner wherever her altars await Him. And all her mystical and actual martyrdoms stream from this living Body. Repeating Christ's Sacrifice, she mediates His action, "the model of that charity which Christ showed us, when He gave Himself up on our behalf, a sacrifice breathing out fragrance as He offered it to God" (Eph. 5:2). Her true center of consciousness, her aspiration, her attitude as she contemplates the world of men she is sent to—all are centered at the altar, stream from the altar, gather again there for the Sacrifice that will bring her desires a definitive fulfillment. The wounds of Jesus are her pulpit; dwelling in them, she gives a new resonance to the words He spoke once to the multitudes of His time. She can say, through His wounds, and across them: "Come to me, all you who labor and are burdened, and I will refresh you." Or again, "If any man thirst, let him come to me and drink." Identified through the Mass continually with His heart, she declares herself as well as Him: "Learn of me, for I am meek and humble of heart. . . ."

Again, through the Mass, the Church is revealed as the nearest witness to the Savior's death; she is, through all the vicissitudes of the centuries, the one authentic voice telling what His death means. At the Mass she stands, not beside the cross of Jesus, as Mary did, but in His very wounds. And since she reenacts Calvary, and hears the resonance of the pierced Heart of the Savior, she alone can really be said to know what passes there. From this supreme vantage point in human and divine history, she can look two ways.

First of all, contemplating that Sacred Heart itself, in the very action which created her, she "is strengthened through His spirit

with a power that reaches her innermost being" (Eph. 3:17 ff.).
Dwelling in the Heart of the Master, all her life is "rooted in love,
founded on love." It is only she who can measure "in all its breadth
and length and height and depth, the love of Christ, to know what
passes knowledge . . . filled with all the completion God has to
give. . . ." Her first view from the altar is of that divine charity
which was the motive of her creation: she looks on the heart of
God Himself, perpetually bringing about on her altars the new creation which bore her. It can be rigorously said that at the Mass the
Church sees God, not as a nude essence, but as a transforming
Savior, an Incarnate Savior Who continues until the end to impreg-
nate and divinize men.

But the Church at the altar is not lost in God, in the sense that
she has forgotten the men for whom she was created. From the
wounds of the Savior, through and in them, she looks outward to
the needs of souls, and the price that must be paid for the continuing
redemption. Her altar, with the Crucified raised above it, is the axis
of the world; from it, in the very humanity of Him Whom she immolates, she hears the cry of that single man spoken of by Augustine
—a cry which reaches even to the Blessed Trinity and the eternal
love that issued in the Incarnation. It is from her altar that the
Church gains her wise perspective of eternity and of time; to dwell
in time by faith, but drawing human aspiration toward the eternity
of her Head and her glorified members: to respect time, neither
wasting nor cluttering it, but continually redeeming it. It is the
tension of this simultaneous consciousness—a purposeful life in time,
an aspiration toward eternity—that gives such a depth, an aspect
of age and wisdom, to her dealings with men. She steps from the altar
with the aura of eternity on her face. And, fortified with the Blood
of the Savior, she reenters the world, for the work appointed her.

But it would be truer to say that even while most active, most
agonized, most preoccupied with the temporal, she had never for a
moment left her altar of adoration and sacrifice. Somewhere, on an
altar known only to her, one of her priests is celebrating; in her name,
with the powers she has granted him, doing, as his intention most
indicates, what the Church intends to do. And because he is at
sacrifice, she is there also; if she were not there his action would be

useless. In the text of her Mass book is the call that summons her, redeemed and redeeming, to the altar; the voices of her virgins, martyrs, and confessors; the intentions of her Pope, her bishops, her living and dead members; her conscious link with the past recalled again, in Abel and Abraham and Melchisedech, her summoning of the angels to adore what her priesthood accomplishes. She has conquered time, she has conquered space, she asserts the power of her altar over death, over the unborn, over the whole communion of saints. They are to come, to kneel, to witness Calvary reenacted. They gather invisibly in a common atmosphere of charity, to the Event that will not die, that refuses to die, that is exactly the same through all centuries, that accomplishes precisely what it first set out to do in the world; unhurried, sure, mysterious, unfailing.

Again, as the Church adores the immolated Body of the Savior on her altars, she has a source of contemplation that forever deepens her understanding of herself. She offers the sacrifice of the Body of her Savior, and she is reminded that for all time she will remain a suffering Body, charged with the dolorous burden of dispensing His Blood through time, reminding the world by her continual death of the death of the Savior. Through the Mass, she understands that the Passion of Christ is not given into her hands as a memory, as an abstraction, as a dead event; but the death she reenacts enters painfully into her own members; she becomes progressively what she immolates; the Victim, the One ordained to die for souls: witness, martyr, interpreter, lover; once seen, her features remind men of the dying face of the Savior. One would hesitate to say it, if it were not an echo of Paul; it is through the Mass that she assumes the form of a slave . . . that she bears about in her body the wounds of the Lord Jesus. In the Mass she finds strength to be considered as nothing, to be set at naught to die; to face tranquilly a human history which has dealt with her exactly as it dealt with her Master.

And yet, it is precisely through the Mass that she radiates glory: "So mindful, Lord, of the passion, resurrection and ascension of Our Lord Jesus Christ . . ." In the Mass is gathered and concentrated all her hope for a future union with the Body she immolates. The eternity she awaits is no mirage, but already a seminal possession, already circulating at her heart and giving her an indestructible growth—the glorious Body and Blood of her Savior. It is eternity that the Mass bells announce. She of all the living will be the witness of the second coming of the Savior. She was born of His wounds, she bears them unhealed in the world; it is through them He will recognize her as His own: "See my hands and my feet." And until that meeting, her hope is the only living thing among men, founded through all time on that Body which she raises above her altars, the Body that will be all of heaven, all of eternity for her. For her whole life and love have been Himself, "that Word Who is life." She will possess Him forever, having tirelessly repeated in the world "what He was from the first, what we have heard about Him" at Bethlehem, at Calvary, in the garden of the Resurrection, on her daily altars, it is He that "met our gaze, and the touch of our hand."

X
Fulness

One has no hope of understanding the Church if he has misunderstood Christ. The two mysteries are parallel, for the Church is the fullness of the Risen Christ extended into time and place. Through the Church, Christ lives on and acts in the world, in spite of time and change—in spite of the completion of His earthly cycle, which has brought His humanity into the glory of the Father. So the Church is created in the image of a God Who lowered Himself, Who dwelt among men and continues to affect men through the human.

The marks of the Church, her holiness, unity, catholicy, apostolicity, come to us through the visible, the human. And here precisely is the scandal. How much easier to believe in God than in Christ; in the Eternal, the Necessary, the All Powerful, instead of submitting to this Form of weakness, of our humanity. And in regard to the Church, how much easier to submit to an invisible society of saints, of the elect, the eternally faithful, instead of this form of the temporal, the victim. How much more satisfactory if human pride can take an immediate leap into the infinite, can have done with human ministers, with mediators, with visible signs, with social obligations to a body of lowliness that cannot match the stride of the impatient and distrustful. Yet precisely this is demanded; just as man reaches the Father through the physical Body of Christ, so he is to reach the Father through the mystical Body of Christ.

If one considers in particular the mark of catholicism, he is face to face with the paradox of a living organism, which suffers the wounds of its passage to the Father, and is still the definitive, the perfect, the Body destined to glory, the Body already bearing the seed of glory. But it is the notion of the Body which scandalizes; as the physical Body of Christ was a scandal to the Docetists, the mystical Body is a scandal to the non-believer today.

The physical Body of Christ was a scandal. Who could accept, without a gift of faith from the Father, this spectacle of the image of His glory, His substance, His name, the full possession of all that is the Father's, reduced to a human body; the form of a slave? "No one can come to Me unless the Father draw Him." St. Augustine could write:

Arius believed in Christ as a creature; the Father did not draw him, because the one who does not believe the Son equal to the Father does not believe in the Father either. What do you say, Arius? Who is this Christ? No true God, he answers, but one whom God has made. Then the Father has not drawn you; you deny His Son. You are dreaming up something else; not the Son; nor are you drawn to the Son, nor is the Father drawing you. For the Son is someone entirely other than what you declare Him. Again, Photinus says, Christ is only a man; He is no God. The one who believes this is not drawn by the Father. Whom then does the Father draw? The one who says, "Thou are the Christ, the Son of the living God. . . ."

And it is the Incarnate Word Who fulfills to the letter the plenitude which the Father wills to transfer to the Church, His Mystical Body. Christ is the Catholic, par excellence, the Incarnation of the Father's plenitude. He is come from what heights ("Being God, thinking it not robbery to be equal to God"; Deum de Deo, lumen de lumine) to what depths of the human situation ("He took the form of a slave. . . . He descended into hell"). He has also become the "universal man" of Augustine's phrase ("He is the cause of salvation to all those who believe; . . . He is the head of the Church; He is the Firstborn of all creatures") Who realizes in Himself an eternal present ("In the beginning the Word already was"), Whose eternity is a solemn reminder of the weight He attaches to time ("Who shall judge the living and the dead"): in Whom are fulfilled the noblest functions of human nature; offices which stood forth in the splendor of His Incarnation, which had existed or would exist only in relation to Him (priest forever according to Melchisedech; prophet—come not to destroy but to fulfill: king, whose Kingdom is not of this world; bridegroom, issuing as a spouse from the bridal chamber; even athlete, exulting like a giant for the running of his course). Who in an eternity forever coexistent with man's present, exercises on him a divinizing action; ["I am with you all days"]; conferring upon those who wayfare the gift of His Spirit, as advocate and teacher ("I will send you another comforter . . . the Spirit of truth, Who will teach you all truth"); the gift of His Body and Blood ("Do this in commemoration of me"); the gift of His mother ("son, behold thy mother"); having placed man forever upon the right road ("I am the Way") has indicated the Term to be arrived at: the Term Who is a Person ("be ye perfect, then, as your heavenly Father is perfect").

So the creation of the Church was the communication of the fullness, the catholicity of the Word Incarnate, to men. St. Paul is at pains to clarify the fact; the Church is the outpouring in time, on a human family, of Him Who dwells from eternity with the Father. "It was his loving design, centered in Christ, to give history its fulfillment by resuming everything in Him, all that is in heaven, all that is on earth, summed up in Him. . . . In Him it was our lot to be called, singled out beforehand to suit His purpose. . . . We were to manifest His glory. . . ."

"It was God's good pleasure to let all completeness dwell in Him, and through Him to win back all things, whether in heaven or on earth, into union with Himself. . . . Now He has used Christ's natural Body to win you back. . . ."

"In Christ the whole plenitude of the deity is embodied, and dwells in Him; and it is in Him that you find your completion. . . ."

The catholicity of the Church, then, as a quality, as a mark of her nature, is hers because of the Divine fullness of Christ, Whose Mystical Body she is. Her catholicity is that expanding fullness of life, at ease in time and in eternity, by which she can claim all men and everything in man to herself. Catholicity is not to be thought of as a mere closed circle of this or that dimension, an idealized humanism in which humanity comes on a Dionysian fullness. Catholicity is a Person, possessed by the Church and possessing her; it is a life which she is granted and has the power of granting. Her catholicity is perhaps best considered as a great universe of all possible fullness: freedom, self-possession, integrity of heart, mutual presence; above all, charity—an infinite enclosure in which the individual Catholic and the whole Mystical Body move and have their being. One might illustrate her riches by choosing a figure from the natural world in which man moves, and say: There is a correspondence, an alliance, between the forces of nature and the catholicity of grace.

For man is, first of all, Catholic in a natural sense. He possesses himself totally, in a unified act that enables him to hold both his thought and himself as thinking subject, in a single act. His sense of reality is acute and vivid, whether he takes in hand a glass of water, or hears a bird suddenly and unexpectedly in the spring, or contemplates a flower. All the world comes home to him; it is his; he receives a complex of sense impressions, reactions, the stimuli of thought and the instinctive movement to possess, like a very king; all things belong to him; they are for his use; he is to make of them what he will. With the greatest gifts of life it is the same; he can experience at any moment friendship, love, literature; they exist for him, to be reacted upon, to form him, to extend the noble light of his personality. He is then first of all Catholic in himself; a universe, a center of judgment and discernment. Gerard Hopkins wrote something of this experience in his notebook:

I find myself, both as man and as myself, something most determined and distinctive, at pitch, more distinctive and higher pitched than anything else I see; I find myself with my pleasures and pains, my powers and my experiences, my desserts and guilt, my shame and sense of beauty, my dangers, hopes, fears, and all my fate, more important to myself than anything else I see. And when I ask where does all this throng and stack of being, so rich, so distinctive, so important, come from—nothing I see answers me . . . that taste of myself, of I and me above and in all things, which is more distinctive than the taste of ale or alum, more distinctive than the smell of walnutleaf or camphor, and is incommunicable by any means to another man: nothing else in nature comes near this unspeakable stress of pitch, distinctiveness, this selfbeing of my own. . . .

And secondly, and especially today, man is naturally catholic in the world, catholic in relation to the world of men. If one stops and takes a contemplative look about him, at how far men have got, even in one lifetime, in spite of the wars and hatred and moral losses of fifty years, he is struck to the heart by the longing of men for catholicity; a longing which simply has not existed before in the world. Man wishes to belong to man, to share the fate of man, to be all men; a catholicity flawed and scarred, marked by tentativeness as well as assurance, by selfishness as by love, by the necessity of a common survival as well as a generous idealism; but still a sense of common destiny, common birth, common needs and hopes. From whom could one have hoped to hear, fifty short years ago, the following statement?

It is disturbing to have lost the feeling of belonging to one reassuring community; to New England, or the United States or to western civilization; it is a lonely and alarming business to feel oneself one in a creation of billions; but it is exciting and inspiriting to be among the first to hail and accept the only fraternal community that can finally be valid—that painfully emerging unity of those who live on the one inhabited star.

No one has regarded the phenomenon of emerging natural catholicism with greater joy and encouragement than Pius XII; his concern for an end of personal and national selfishness was woven into many of his public statements of the past ten years. What makes this one remarkable is the insistence on a law of catholicity present in the social organism:

The clear fact that relations between individuals of various nations, and between nations themselves, are growing in multiplicity and intensity makes daily more urgent the right ordering of international relations . . . all the more so since this mutual drawing together is caused not only by vastly improved technological progress and by free choice, but also by the more profound action of an intrinsic law of development. This movement then is not to be repressed, but fostered and promoted.

Catholicity, naturally speaking, is the sense of self-possession, and of possession of the world. And the supernatural idea of catholicism is illuminated from the natural analogy. The Catholic possesses himself more surely, possesses an infinitely larger universe, than the natural man. One might break the analogy into its components, borrowing from natural creation, and say: As a Catholic, a member of the Body of Christ, with a grasp on the "holos," the whole of reality, the believer too has his atmosphere, prayer—his nourishment, the Eucharist; his light, God's presence; his companionship, the community of all men in Christ; and, moving closer to the person, to the possession of man by himself in his psychological catholicity; he has an interior sense-life, the exemplarity of Christ and the saints impinging on Him; his mind is the self-consciousness of the Church, its power of synthesizing reality for him; this plus the absolute assurance it gives that what it reveals is true, that it can neither deceive nor be deceived. Finally; the infused gift of love, a supernatural heartbeat that will still be pulsing in eternity, unchanging in its object and intensity. . . .

There is simply no end in sight, then, to the vastness of the universe possessed by the Catholic. Claudel can write:

From now forward, we do not make use only of our forces to love, to understand, to serve God; but in one act we make use of all things; from the Queen of heaven and earth down to the poor leprous African with the little bell in hand, breathing out the responses of the Mass through a mouth half-fallen away. All of creation, visible and invisible, all history, all the past, all the present and future, all of nature, all the treasures of the saints multiplied by grace, all this is at our disposition, all this is our prolongation. We can make use of the intelligence of St. Thomas, of the right arm of St. Michael, of the heart of Joan of Arc and of Catherine of Sienna and all hidden resources which we need merely to touch in order to make them flow in our direction. Everything good, everything great and beautiful from one end of the earth to the other, this is our own work. The heroism of the missionaries, the inspirations of the holy learned, the generosity of the martyrs, the genius of artists, the fervent prayer of the little Clares and the Carmelites, it is as though it were ourselves; it is ourselves! From north to south, from alpha to omega,—we put all of these things into action. . . . Breathing, circulation, the balance of possession and duty, everything that in the individual body is entrusted to the cells,—all this finds its analogy in this immense circumference of Christianity. Everything that is in us, even without our being conscious of it, the Church translates and paints outside us on a scale of absolute magnificence. Outside of us, at astronomical distances, we discern the same texts that are traced microscopically in the depths of our hearts.

The Catholic is in the Church; it is the Church which makes him Catholic, a whole, a perfect thing. The Church comes before the unregenerate soul whose description was written so tellingly by St. Paul in his letter to the Romans; confronts the soul with the full- ness of Christ, ready, powerful to apply it all, to mediate faith, hope, charity to the needy one. And man today comes into the Church in exactly the same sense as Augustine or Thérèse entered; the same ineffable "drawing" is exercised by the Father in his direction; once the ontological bond was established, these saints were Christ's; so is the new member. There is one Head of all, one source of all grace, from which all have drawn.

And if there is distinction among the ordinary members, let it be only of holiness; and if it is of holiness, let it be secret until the end. God alone shall judge. In the meantime, apparent diversity, differences of works, of nationality, of natural gifts, have been brought to a fulness, have been unified in a common love and effort. Drawn once into the Body, they have been consecrated to the uses of the whole Body. There shall be, for one's exclusive credit, for his pride or ambition, no longer one work or another, one nation or another, one age or condition and another; for the unction of the Holy Spirit has reached to the last member of the Body; all are consecrated; all have something personal to contribute, something otherwise un- suppliable toward the building up of the whole. Can one then be honored, and one despised? The idea is intolerable to him who feels in his marrow the common lifeblood of the Eucharist inflaming all the Body, the excellence of that undivided Spirit speaking and acting through Christ's members.

Would it not be useful to reflect too at this point that the catholicity of the Church is compatible with the presence of the partial, the wounded, the limited; compatible even with a lack of vision, of productivity; with sinfulness and weakness, with all the

litany of human evils and failings? Grace has not come to create the
superman; the greatness of the Church is not her ability to erase
wounds but to assume them, to use them as Christ did before her;
to live with them, to be patient under them, to work in spite of, sometimes because of, them.

A program of escape the Church has never embraced. Her way
to catholicity, to the readying of men for eternity, is through the
cross, through death. She has no other path to glory except that
marked out for her by the footsteps of the Son of God. Who has
ever heard on her lips, in her Gospel or liturgy or preaching, such
words as appear like a corrupting stain on the fabric of other religions: norvana, carnal reincarnation, worldly success a sign of pre-
destination, naturalistic optimism? Against all these her voice is
grave, demanding, rigorous: "Take up your cross and follow me.
. . . The man who does not despise his life, loses it. . . . Unless the
seed falls to the earth and dies, itself remains alone. . . . Unless you
all shall do penance, you shall perish. . . . He who loves not his
brother and says he loves God, is he not a liar?"

The problem of the relation of human weakness to the fullness
of Christ in His Church becomes even more neuralgic if one considers the presence of sin among believers. It is a fact, illustrated by
the parables of Christ, that sin grows and comes to harvest in the
Kingdom along with the fruit of the good seed. The Church knows
it; there are in her midst ineffectual lives buried under layers of
passion, self-indulgence, pride, blindness: stifled lives, unable to live
and unable to escape life; a kind of life in death, where the friendship between Christ and man, implied in the call to baptism, is never
quite broken and yet never reaches its term of strength. But the
Church hopes on, for even sin can have a kind of value in reverse.
Sin serves her, as it served Him; "Sin in the world is the slave who
draws up from the well, the waters of life." O *felix culpa!* She has
found no good reason to omit the exultant cry from her liturgy; she
sings it not only to recall the Savior, but remembering her own
contemporary sufferings, remembering what sin is doing to her today;
O *felix culpa!* Sins of hatred give her her martyrs. Sins of impurity
release into a stronger, fiercer light the purity of her virgins. Sins of
blindness and calumny excite in her body those sublime reactions of

Christ before the court: "He said nothing; He was as a lamb before the shearer." Sins of blasphemy and cursing make rise to God, all the purer and more interior, all the more determined and steady and knowledgeable, the praise of the Mass and the Divine Office, the Catholic life of reparation, whose intensity and fervor offer Him more than the betrayer could ever steal from Him. . . .

And what of the sinful Catholic? Can one speak in any real sense of his possession of fullness in grace, fullness in love, fullness in life? He appears not very different from a man who has no help from God, who has little faith, little charity; immersed in the world, living for time; reacting with disgust and irritation to anything beyond the minimal in sacrifice or personal commitment. What is the Church to make of him, in face of the dynamism of Catholic fulness? Where does the abundant life promised by Christ invade this life?

The answer is, of course, that one must not attempt an answer. For a double mystery is implied here: the mystery of a choice of God according to the measure of His gift of grace, and the mystery of a human response. One approaches the problem of the failings of others most honestly, with greatest hope of an answer, when he immediately relates them to his own sins. Reflection on one's own refusals opens up vividly the mystery of human malice and weakness. On the other hand, if one persists in considering evil only as an extrinsic phenomenon, as something foreign, a matter of speculation, he misses the depth and breadth and height of the compassion and mercy of Christ. But if he has courage to consider himself, a man arrives at some reflections which, though not definitive to the mystery of evil, are still of importance.

Sin still serves. In the individual life, if one may so speak, it is sin that saves from greater sin. The memory of carnal sin saves from spiritual sin. The state of penitence makes improbable the state of final impenitence. And again, there is a great uncharted fullness possible to the saint who has arisen from sin; how attractive, how accessible his example seems to others! By the divine mercy, and in no sense implying that sin is anything but an unmitigated evil, it can still be said: the example of the penitent saves the Church, in the honor and welcome she offers him, from the least taint of pharisaism, from the charge of angelism. It is not sin one extols here; it is the triumph of grace, which has won the victory of accepting human life as it is, without dislocating its identity, and which with an infinite compassion has bidden it arise from the dead.

The presence of sin, then, will never be incompatible with the presence of the infinitely holy Christ, in His Church. One could even say that if sin were imperiously exiled from her presence, the Church would not be the Church of her Master, but a kind of transplanted angelic choir. If she is to be Catholic in the sense that her heart goes out to all, she must at the same time tolerate sin, in the hope of forgiving it. If she is to heal the wounds of men, she must assume them. If she is to restore the sinner, she must welcome him. And one of the most glorious aspects of her claim to the fullness of Christ is exactly this, that she has not cast the sinner forth, she has not increased the number of the world's hopeless, the world's rejected; her compassion still goes out to all men, to any man, reminding him that the grounds for the world's judgments are never hers; that she knows, of all the vast catalogue of her history, in all those centuries of guilt that have been whispered to her in secret—of all this, she has never found the sin she could not deal with; the sin that was too great, too cancerous, too deeply rooted, that could not be torn up, could not be exorcised. The Church does not seek the dubious human prerogative of remaining pure by not allowing evil to approach her. It is her glory, one of the marks of her Divine origin, that she suffers evil because she alone can erase it. It were easy to claim holiness because in secret one did not know how to deal with evil, one was scandalized by it, one was powerless and in fear of it; such an idea of purity would be only constricting, inhuman, powerless. What makes the Church the source of all fullness, all holiness, is this, that her love has never in the history of the world known a human measurement, a hypocritical reaction, a determination to limit love, to exclude from her love.

Also acute, when confronted with the ideal of catholicity, is the presence of intellectual and moral blindness in the Church. In many areas where legitimate human development is at stake, in the battle for the rights of the underprivileged, the poor, those of another color or race, the Catholic conscience has not always been conspicuous for bravery or enlightenment. And the questions arise; Where are the social effects of grace? Where is that pure outpouring, into the totality of human life, of the gifts of the Spirit sung at Pentecost?

"Wash Thou what is stained with sin, water what is dry within, heal Thou what is wounded sore. Bend Thou what is stiff of will, warm Thou what with cold is chill, guide Thou what has strayed before."

In how many cases, believers must admit to their shame that the works of the Holy Spirit, meant to be accomplished with Him and in Him, have been done only because liberalism of spirit and natural charity take the risks which the cowardice of the Christian conscience has refused. One must admit that the holy fire of the Spirit is carefully banked in many hearts, in many institutions of the Church; banked under years of traditional thinking and inaction, unwilling to emerge into the light and suffer the impact of scrutiny and the need of change; not anxious to restore all things in Christ, but persisting unchanged because vested interests not always coincident with the interests of Christ are imperiled by the call to change; contented with a minimal application of truth to life, suspicious of youth, ignoring the evident need for reform, substituting a minimal appeal to justice for the reign of charity. The problem is so large, so unpleasant, so terrifying, that even an admission of its existence is not always welcome. It were better, one would almost conclude, to consider Catholic wholeness only as a thing apart, a matter of unapplied truth, a charity chained to the altar, a faith which dreads to be put to the test. But such a mentality must face a choice: either one will put the gifts of the Spirit to work in the world as it exists, or he will strive to wrench the Spirit of Christ from the Body of Christ, subconsciously leading the retreat of the Body, its recession; dreaming of a Church of bodiless worship, cut off from street and market and factory, without a part in the great decisions that alter the face of time and lead humanity to victory or disaster; a Church rather dismembered than whole, more abstract than real, the merest shadow of a Presence.

The Church announced by the Gospel is other than this. One does not have to set up his mental dwelling in the past in order to love the Church; but a viable love of her will dwell in all her great days, past and present, when her mind, that mind of Christ Jesus, is the leaven of human life, when her conscience issues in action that is worthy of the best of man's potential. Action in public; a Church whose countenance is visible, whose voice is heard; the cry is that of Christ, of Peter, of the Papal social tradition flowering wonderfully in Pius XII. A program of social reform clearly expounded and unequivocally accepted; words that are not merely admired but followed through to their last demand; programs not enshrined in libraries, or decked out for public occasions where lip service becomes a way of implicitly neglecting their everyday application. But public occasions rather signalize the corporate determination that the years, the days, the buying and selling and recreation and work, home and school and marriage, youth and maturity, are integrally dedicated to the Christian task, now and then pause to take stock of themselves, to gather common inspiration, to give public notice of what is a daily enterprise, a way of proceeding, a manner of life.

Such is the profound relation between the Christian word and the Christian task. Unless action follows upon thought, it is wonderful and fearful how structures degenerate into a mockery of the truth, how words are emptied, and men eventually persuade themselves that the whole of life can be achieved in a proliferation of schemes, programs, organizations, manifestoes. But the soul of thought, its test, its genuine will to make a difference in life, depends upon the living nourishment it is drawing from previous action, and the will it transmits to further action.

At the same time that the man of faith courageously faces the human failures in the Mystical Body, he would be guilty of an unwarranted pessimism were he to conclude that there are not miraculous areas of heroism, originality, daring. It is not the coward, the recessionist, the reactionary who represents the Spirit at work, or who is recognized by the Church, ultimately, as bearing her Spirit, as her man of wholeness. The formula that raises men and women to the altars is, as it has always been, martyr, apostle, hero, lover. The nearer one approaches the beating heart of the Church, the fullness of her life incarnate in human life, the nearer he approaches the single word "saint." And studying the saints, reading their words, one has before him the living text of the Gospel spirit; he is able, no matter how defeating or discouraging his experience has been elsewhere, to experience again the definition of the Church in action; the gift, with perseverance and enthusiasm and an utterly selfless love, first of the things of God to God, then, with an equal love, of the things of man to man.

And one comes to the conclusion: the more deeply a man is immersed in the Church, is formed by her, to that exact degree will he become a whole man; whole in his love of God, whole in his agonized labor for justice in life, whole in his social attitudes, whole in his spontaneous reactions, cleanness of heart, the will to peace. It can never be because one is Catholic that he is indifferent toward the persecuted, or a sower of dissention or a perpetuator of inequality; it is in spite of the Church, it is in opposition to her; it is by ignoring her, misreading her, refusing to give her a hearing. For the Incarnation that has given birth to the Church means not only that Divinity was visibly present in the world; it means that Divinity has embraced the human; it means that humanity has received an imperious call to the Divine. It means that whatever is good in nature, whatever noble, whatever lovely, is of concern to the Church, her field of labor; that wherever an area of injustice is sown with tares, she will work to clear it; that conditions intolerable to human dignity, to peace and unity, are alike a scandal to her pure and courageous eyes. One must never tire of repeating: she gazes with the human and compassionate glance of Christ upon the sufferings of men; and she will expend her last strength, her last word, to heal them.

If a man would call himself Catholic, let him take the Catholic Church as she is, or let him depart from her, but let him never commit the supreme folly of trying to remake her to an image of malice or blindness or self-interest. Let him work with her, or oppose her, but let him not deceive himself, and shame her name before men, by saying that a third course is possible; that she condones him, or that he represents her. "Let your speech be yea yea and nay nay"; and your actions too. . . .

In turning the pages of the New Testament, one has a constant evidence that the Church, continuing the mission of Christ, has a duty of restoring, increasing, perfecting the mark of catholicity in

the souls and bodies of men; in social life, as in man's secret con-
sciences; wherever eternal life is in jeopardy because time is being
vitiated or exploited or wasted. "To recapitulate all things in Christ";
to sum them up, to perfect the rough copy of creation, to give
mankind and his world a presentable final form, writing between the
lines of human biographies, the word which gives man his meaning:

Why, you yourselves are the letter we carry about with us, written in
our hearts, for all to recognize and read. You are an open letter from
Christ, promulgated through us; a message written not in ink, but in the
spirit of the living God, with human hearts, instead of stone, to carry
it. . . .

What has been wrenched asunder by sin, reduced to a scattered
ruin, is again restored by Christ: "It is in Him you find your completion." And this completion is expressed in a figure that says everything, that is as daring as it is true: "You are the Body of Christ."
So there is a further step; those who join the Church undertake her
mission: Christ Who came to redeem, to buy back in His Blood, has
made all believers into redeemers through the anointing of baptism;
they are baptized into the Body, perfected in the Body, joined to It
for the sake of those who are near and those who are far off. Christ
the physician has healed the human race; He has made those He
has healed into sources of healing for the world. Christ has forgiven
men; it is so that the idea of forgiveness may take root in man's dealings with men: "Forgive us our trespasses, as we forgive those who
trespass against us." He has restored their sight; but as a social bene-
fit, since if the blind walk with the blind, both shall fall into the
ditch. He has healed the halt, not alone to enable them to walk, but
to make them into bearers of the burdens of others.

The Catholic, then, is in the Church, a whole, a perfect creation;
and being wedded to her, flesh of her flesh, he is made perfect also;
is given the only possibility of a perfection that transcends time. If
the first statement is true: the Catholic is in the Church, a second
one must follow: the whole Church is in the Catholic. The fullness
of heaven descends to him, as though he were the final word of the
Creator, as indeed he is. In Christ, the Godhead descends to each;
God made into the form of a slave, born of a woman, born in time,

to be made available, to make it possible for God to reach within, to enter, to touch, to transform. And for those born after His historical course is finished, there abides the Church, visibly present as Christ was, to do for man what He did once for all on Calvary. The whole Church is in the individual soul—certainly according to an analogy; there are different offices, there are different dignities in the body—but in all that relates to catholicity, to the fullness of Christ, the members share in an equal dignity; simply, in the grace of the Redeemer. In heaven, all offices of the Church will disappear; Pope and hierarchy and sacraments and a priesthood offering its sacrifice; faith will have been swallowed in vision, hope in fulfillment; the only possession that will cross the horizon into eternity is charity. It is charity upon which men must finally take a stand; the vocation, the life of each, the substance of all the Church has to offer. Père de Lubac writes: "Christianity does not recognize among its members any difference such as those that hold among other sects. . . . there is no such thing as 'hearer and elect'; as believers and the perfect. In all the differences of their offices and employment, all are ruled, in the following of the same Christ, by the same spiritual law. All have part in the same life; all rejoice in the same grace and the same sacraments, in line with the same destiny; 'all are endowed with the same grandeur and the same nobility, conferred by the same precious Blood of Christ.' (Pius XI)"

This is true enough, and well enough known. What is not stressed so often is the painful paradox; the Church restores the soul, heals it, by wounding it. She makes it Catholic by making the Passion of Christ operate in it. There are no exemptions from suffering among those who love her best; in fact, the highest meaning of the word "chosen" in her vocabulary is: chosen for suffering as the way to glory. Through the sacraments, through her prayer and the supreme act of the Mass, she releases the inner meaning of suffering; what could only afflict, deaden, destroy, and blight human life enters the cycle of the Savior; from the cross to glory. She has made suffering into a kind of sacrament, a visible sign of grace. It is not the blind mechanism of an indifferent or cruel God; it is the painful threshing floor, the furnace, where the personality emerges, purified, worthy to live and to die, its inner order restored, the wound of nature subdued, the body made into a fit companion for eternal life.

XI

The Kingdom

The Old Testament had foreshadowed; the New would not hesitate to insist on it: the way to eternal life lies through a cleansing of heart, a purification to "the joining of body and spirit." Men will live by love, or they will consent that death possess the race of men. The opposite of love is nothing so harmless as the unwillingness to love; it is the destruction of the person: and from that, the rotting and falling apart of all the public fabric, the clothing life wears. Life without hope, without responsibility, without civic sense; a puerile religion with a father image for its totem; marriage endured like an armed neutrality. Since love, like water, must flow freely, when the pressure of love or water is enclosed, enforced, stemmed, it will seek any escape from the intolerable necessity of non-love, the pressure of standing still, a dead weight like a corpse. "Give me an out," is the cry of love. "Give me another person."

Christians are called to be experts in love, professional men and women of love. Does not the hope of the Kingdom start with the individual? If only each is sincerely Christian, into public life issue the poor of heart, the peacemaker, the clean of mind and soul and heart, the merciful (especially, and first of all, toward one another), the patient, those who hunger and thirst after justice. Apart from this will toward sincerity, the Kingdom remains enshrined in books, on the lips of priests, a buried treasure.

It is worth asking: What would happen if people began generally living in this way, by the Christian blueprint? Perhaps it is useless to dream of large conquests until the Kingdom has a few wholly purified people, detached from the things of this world, living in simplicity of heart and love for one another, and a healthy, humorous indifference to group pressure; who in this way make Christianity attractive, workable, available, who make others pause in their course because they have caught this unmistakable, elusive cachet of holiness. God has come to earth to set the stage for heaven here and now. Man is not summoned into a future unrelated to the present; people who will know Him in eternity are those who know Him in time, and know the meaning of time. The Kingdom of God is within you. The beatitudes, in their insistence on sincerity, in their probing of the heart as to its interior quality, give men something more than a hint of the kind of men and women who will win eternal life. The first act is part of the drama. In substance, heaven is now, if faith means anything. Those who are building the Kingdom will find themselves no stranger to the atmosphere of eternity; they acclimatize themselves to it now. A home, a religious community that reflects the beatitudes, a Christian sense of work and recreation: these things have eternity at their core. The sword that Christ came to wield is not to deal its blow in severing the Kingdom on earth from the Kingdom of heaven; He strikes rather between the "world" and the Kingdom; and in so doing unites heaven with earth.

This Kingdom has a long history. The Garden of Eden saw its beginning; a social and personal state of things where God and the Divine life were the measure of all things. Paradise said, "The Kingdom of God is come upon you." Fidelity to God would have made it definitive, permanent: but its survival always depended upon a choice. Another way of saying, God had too much respect for the work of His hands merely to impose the Kingdom on men and women. Paradise was not to be an innocence without cost, without commitment; men had to pay for it: choose! And they chose wrong; because Satan had plans for a Kingdom too, and both God and Evil had this in common; they realized the Kingdom was to be primarily a spiritual state of things, stemming from a viable choice; and both God and Satan, being great, were impatient to rule. . . . Choose me, or choose Me . . . and men chose. From now until the Incarnation, the Kingdom would exist independently of material circumstance; now in poverty, again, in freedom from want; when the prophets were heard, or when they were persecuted; when human anguish drove the people further than usury or idolatry or lust could reach, for a light upon life's darkness. In Jerusalem, that city of promise, or by the rivers of Babylon, in mourning for an ancient home. In the desert, scoured by weathers and thirst and hunger, and living day by day on a Providence that refused them security. Or in the early days of the promised land, when wealth had not yet stolen their hearts aside. In a more complicated and ambiguous sense, under David, through his tears and repentance, under the aegis of a king who was fully human, now and then a committed rebel, and yet never corrupted by the spreading stain of impenitence. Finally, under the burden of building the temple of Jehovah; a common cause of worship and enthusiasm and praise; to gather the riches of the earth so that the Lord might be honorable among His people.

In brief years such as these, one notes a common cause in God's favor; a conscious impulse in one direction, extending its light into every area of living; a will to accept the consequences of God's existence, to live in integrity, to eradicate sin, root and branch, through penance and prayer; to live not by morality or decency or any other substitute; but simply because God was the Lord, and the people His possession. An immense social grace rewove the fabric of life from its very thread; to purify conscience, to live in public as one lived at heart; a public life that was at the same time profoundly personal, because social duties were seen ultimately as acts of service and adoration of the Most High God. One notes, too, the delicate interplay of social conditions with the spiritual estate of the people; so complicated, so unpredictable a mutual effect that one cannot declare what precise historical conditions will best bring the Kingdom to pass. At peace in homeland, or in growing national glory, under the young Solomon. In the voice of the prophets, honored and heard; in the vicious limepits and fields of blood where the nation killed its great men and stilled, by blasphemy, desecration and murder, the possibility of a divine visitation. By sorrow for sin, by consciousness of sin expiated; at any hour, to any place, among any generation, the Lord might come. For in every case, God vindicated His freedom. Grace was not to be delimited by what men would declare God capable of. He would come when He would. He would sweep aside, with a stroke of invincibility, with a simple fiat of His upraised arm, human predication, human exigence. It was He, finally, Who would declare and affirm what soil was readied for him, and what sour and stony; what tree would be cursed and what would yield. He would give the victory, and give the defeat; and then show, by the dolorous overturn of both, that victory was defeat and defeat victory; that exile was home, since He was pleased to be present there, and that the Kingdom of earth was indeed an unbearable exile, since He would abominate it. Let men distrust and find tricky the easy human words "victory," "prestige," "a great name"; let them live in fear and trembling, since only He knew whether behind the scenes the truth awaited a hearing, or poison and death lurked.

Finally, the Word was made flesh, and dwelt among us. And He announces, as the event of His coming had announced before He opened His mouth to speak: The Kingdom of God has come among you. Not in a figure of speech, not in a hero standing up to set things aright, to teach this or that lesson that would effect a change of heart in the direction of God. But in fact: in Me. Not because a human radiance of leadership and greatness, compounded in one irresistible moment of time, has made the Kingdom seem again, temporarily, wonderfully possible. Not because a movement of enthusiasm has swept tired impossibilities from the heart of man, and he finds that in the vigor of that voice he can begin again his dolorous trek, with new heart and energy. No: the moment has come. The substance of the Kingdom is among you in its King. "Touch me and see that it is I." Or again, it is "what our eyes have seen, and our ears heard, and our hands touched, of the word of life."

The Kingdom is announced, because its King is present. Let there be no stretching of hand or heart into the impossible, into the future, into escape. The human order, established by grace, and made radiant in the presence of the Divine, the unutterable, the utterly Other, is among you. Humanity's hour has struck. Will the

notes of that sublime hour, the substance of waiting and tears
and prayer and martyrdom and poetry, be heard in the march of
armies, or among a people that can speak with pride of their centuries of unbroken fidelity? It will not. He has come not with sword
in hand; He is Himself the sword; and the stroke of His healing blow
sets free the new earth for the sake of a new heaven. An enslaved
people, a low point of legalism and external observance in religious
life; the poverty of a workman's village; the battle is joined. It is
joined, not because of arbitrary circumstances of a given point of
history, but because a people, priest and wealthy and poor alike,
were determined that they alone would set the circumstances under
which the Kingdom would be accepted; what character the Kingdom
would assume, under what conditions it would be allowed a hearing
or, indeed, survival. Let the King step into this mold, let Him assume this character, or it will not go well with Him; let His Kingdom be of this world.

My Kingdom is not of this world. The announcement nears,
without a hint of its shocking character. "He went up into a mountain side; there He sat down, and His disciples with Him." A scene
of verdent freshness, the sitting of a country preacher for an afternoon of devotion with a crowd of unsophisticated followers. And into
that scene, with its deceptive air of humanity at its best, humanity
undisturbed and at peace, without embroilment of passion or con-
nivance or envy, St. Matthew gathers into one the epitome of the
Kingdom, scattered widely through the discourses of the Savior's
public life. It is an irony that deserves the name Divine. For within
the space of an hour's converse, and in a scene of imperishable freshness verging on the unreal, the sword deals its blow; a tranquil appeal
for men to cast off what has passed for their religious history, as
vested and interpreted in an unworthy leadership; to strike out anew
into a future that leads, directly and imperiously, to Divine life.

The Kingdom has roots in the old covenant; it assumes the pre-
cepts of the old, by enveloping them in an interior spirit. It breathes
life into a procession of the dead. Surely the race of men had not
lived, up to the coming of the Savior, without love? The high tide
of the nation's greatness, whether it was reached in an upper class that
dealt justice to the poor, or a poor nation whose spirit was un-

quenched by slavery and destitution; these had learned love, and practiced love, in the very jaws of hatred. But how circumscribed and how temporary these fine epiphanies had been! If David and Jeremiah and the prophets had given the nation a voice of grandeur and a personal idiom before the God of love, how easily that voice had been drowned by the voices of this world: the code, the commentaries on the code, the refinements of the commentaries. By the seepage of the legalistic into the purity of religious sensibility, this point had been reached; a people who were content to admit love to the basic human relationships: courtship, marriage, childbearing, friendship—but whose thought of love as the power of ascent to God was entirely deadened. "This people serves me with its voice."

Into so infected a bloodstream did the measured, dispassionate voice of the Lord breathe. "I say to you, if your justice does not give fuller measure than the justice of the scribes and the Pharisees, you shall not enter into the Kingdom of heaven." The interior character of God's Kingdom, a love entirely spiritual, a pedagogy by force of which the hour of death will find eternal life recognizable before man's eyes—what has such a plan to do with the legalistic oligarchy set up by the leaders of Israel? The answer, in the Divine voice, is a return to new beginnings; to that imperishable reservoir of love, of good will, of interiority, temporarily sullied by the enemy; but still lying dormant, unslain, awaiting the word that will quicken it again.

The announcement is made. But a simple declaration of intent is not enough; it is only the beginning. For the Kingdom is no sooner born than it is violently set upon. Its infancy, its very presence has about it such an affront to the old ways of men, that where it demands space on the human scene, it is an immediate source of scandal. It must die. It is an evident infamy. The point of the struggle is initiated by our Lord on two fronts: within man and in his social groupings. It is man, first of all, who must do battle in his own members. Cleanness of heart, mercy, poverty of spirit, patience, hungering after justice are not his natural climate. He is by nature a rebel, and the seeds of his revolt, cast broadside into his social life, are within. The war is joined not only in the multitude that presses upon the Master, hearing in His voice the attraction of fearlessness and the native air of truth; it reaches first of all the twelve, as His

own men, those nearest His presence, those burdened with responsibility for the pure transmission of His voice. Will they hear? If
they will, they have declared war.

They have declared war on man, as the dawn of the Kingdom
discovered him. One need only turn to the first chapters of the letter
of Paul to the Romans to discover the full malevolence of that human landscape across which the light of the Kingdom broke. A war
on unregenerate man; a war on man possessed, literally and fearfully,
by the powers of darkness. And from that possession, the brutal
impact of hell is humanized and made palpable in a world claimed
for the possession of evil.

But to His own, in the freshness of a new day, the Lord has
come; He Who through all of recorded history had only spoken
through His prophets or in those momentary visitations of splendor,
now literally "opened His mouth." The Kingdom of God is upon
you. And the Kingdom in its early hours, in the purity of its irresistible religious spirit, carries all before it; from the hour of its
effective birth and mandate, with the experiences of the Lord's death,
resurrection and ascension assimilated to its body and soul; with the
Spirit descended, it bears all the marks of heaven into a world
without hope. Individual responsibility: each member luminous with
the form of the whole social effort; each finally a living text in whom
the Divine intention can be read. A strong social commitment
is the embodiment of an intensely realized union with the Divine.
The social virtues flourish because man is at peace with his own spirit
and with God. The mystical element is strongly in the ascendant; a
holy impatience makes legislation unnecessary; this "first generation
of the promise" senses that the testament is written in its very flesh,
and did it not feel also within it the birth pangs of another and
lesser generation, it would outlaw the law itself. But what counts for
the present is the inner law of charity; so close is the interaction of
nature and grace that it is extremely difficult to know whether the
project is succeeding because of the native integrity of nature, reinforced certainly by grace; or whether grace has quite simply swept
all other considerations before it. The mood is Pentecostal or apocalyptic; it is the moment of the transfiguration—in any case, it is painful to realize that the occasion is momentary, that the bright flame

will settle down, that custom will replace inspiration, and law give a necessary articulation to the spirit, grown more and more self-effacing.

In the beginning, too, a strong apostolicity is instinctive. Those who are launched upon the religious adventure know that the word has reached them precisely as good news; nothing can be concealed; what has grasped them in the privacy of the heart has so subsumed all other values into its supreme one, that the word of love begins to demand a hearing elsewhere. Go and teach. The mystical stage admits of no closed system between spirit and spirit, and would castigate as selfishness the attempt to close ranks or set up distinctions. Where the spirit is abroad, every man is unworthy, and every man is worthy; worthy of the effort of a human love that will open before him the splendor of Divine love.

A characteristic of love which appears clearly in the early stages is that of personal exhilaration. Love, while always rational, and perhaps most perfectly so at this stage, is not yet rationalized; it has not undergone the painful self-scrutiny that will later tend to balance off enthusiasm against cost; and to set up a working compromise. When the goal is clear, the means are secondary; another way of saying that a charism tends to clear the mists of the future, to telescope time, and to make the achieved Kingdom appear very near; very nearly won, just beyond the next effort of love. One has but to cross the threshold, one has but to make an effort which appears paltry in view of the winning; all life can be attained in a moment. And from such a mentality springs, as its own pure outpouring, those efforts of art and literature which express the uncluttered possession of eternity in the present. The resonance of the prayer "Thy Kingdom come" is felt as a present experience, in the body; the eternal is present, the moment has come; men have only to stretch a hand and the transcendent goods are in their grasp. One breathes as the residue of this holy perfume the paintings of Fra Angelico, the mosaics of Ravenna, the abrupt announcements of the early Christian tombs: he has won peace, she is with God.

Also noteworthy in the evolution of the Kingdom in sacred history is this; the process of inner deterioration, marking the course of all human enterprise, never occurs here. Across the broad face of history, and altering its features in spite of age and time and human defilement, comes the constant inner renewal which cannot be explained on any human grounds. One might even say: where the social nature of the Kingdom is most obscured, where the will to defacement and neglect are most vigorous and determined, the Spirit rejoices to put its enemies to confusion once more. Brought to the attention of the Church again and again, and at the cost of personal suffering and death, is the word that men are sinning against the light; set against the mainstream of selfishness is the saint, witnessing that the truth has not died, that the presence of the Master and the Kingdom of his words are still manifest.

And along with the effect of interior renewal, the impulse is outward; the Kingdom is the very opposite of a closed society. Those who live its law in the most interior sense, within the Christian tradition, feel painfully the responsibility to offer it to others. Such responsibility is a common element of Christian mysticism; the secret call that is still a public one; because it refuses to the mystic the luxury of concluding that a Kingdom can come to rest in one person, or that the term of the Church is to be anything less than mankind. One could not hesitate to say, in the case of the great Christian mystics, that their mysticism is an apostolate. Invigorating and giving staying power to their greatest moments of apprehension of God, there runs the constant cry: Thy Kingdom come.

This is true because in the grace that has brought them to the face of God, there comes the quickened apprehension of the creative plan. Nearness to God has caused them to follow the Divine glance to its last object: the salvation of all men. Their act of love has been a choice, but a choice without exclusiveness. It has not rested upon a static Essence, but upon a God Who is the source of all creation; sustaining, directing, willing the salvation of all, impatient until His love had invaded every human heart. In their approach to God was implied the radical truth by which they were sent forth from God; after the image of Him Who, dwelling always with the Father, nevertheless made His dwelling among men, and Who from the midst of the human scene could calmly declare, "I and the Father are one."

The bearers of the Kingdom at its purest and most transcendent form, then, have all of them been men and women of action; a state of things which is comprehensible only to those who can grasp the depth and breadth of the synthesis their lives worked. What but the Divine grace could effect a simultaneous concentration and diffusion of energy, so that God should crown the finest point of consciousness, a point to which all men would be also present? What except grace could extend the reach of men so far, include so many other men in a single life, and still heal all the interstices of ignorance, weakness, blindness, preference, that infect the world with groupings and division?

But the mystical stage recedes; even within the Kingdom, guaranteed the effective presence of the Spirit until the end of days, the fruits of the Spirit will not always be public or extraordinary. Another temptation is tailored for this period, even as implicit in the first was a kind of spiritual simony—to sell the fruits of the Holy Spirit for a gain that could only be ambiguous and doomed; a headline, or a mode of entrance to the great; the opportunity to work miracles before Herod. Now the Master turns to the Kingdom as it will inhabit the earth during the broad sweep of history; largely hidden, leavening in secret, the treasure lying undiscovered in the fields. The temptation at this stage will be, by one means or another, to force the Spirit into the thoroughfare; to give His secret gifts a public face: to perform before men acts which demand by an inner law to please God from the heart. Acts of piety, almsgiving, prayer, fasting: they are the expression of that reverence by which man declares his identity and simultaneously brings it home to his own flesh; to be a creature, to be dependent, to be a member of the militant Kingdom, to be, but for the curb of penance, a source of revolt and passion. But by such acts of adoration, the Kingdom builds its secret tissues and cells, and reminds itself that its vitality can only be protected if men will have the courage to labor in the darkness of faith, to seek no honor except that which comes from God, to value jealously those personal acts which make the Creator present to the creature, and reveal His face in all creation.

Along with these positive acknowledgments of God, also great acts of refusal. My Kingdom is not of this world. It dwells in those who have secretly labored to assimilate the Divine values, and perhaps with no great effort of attention, have refused to yield before

the pressures of the material. They do not fret over needs that are
at best provisory; true needs, but in the score of Christian value, of
no great moment. They have learned to use objects without being
used up; all creation, even the most opaque elements within it, becomes transparent before a gaze that summons, by the very purity
of its regard, the Divine Name. But looking backward to a period of
the Kingdom when life (so one should believe) was more fruitful,
more immersed in the Divine, marked more deeply by recognition
of the values of God—so the forms of the temptation go; a myopia
under history, the lack of a simple balance of spirit before God,
not allowing Him to decree or allow the general character of this
or that age, not learning from the past its own best lesson: that
conditions upon earth were never more than an approximation of
the ideal; and that the best guarantee that the Kingdom is present
now is the willingness of the members to work for it under God's
present manifestation of providence.

Prayer, almsgiving, fasting: these are not mere borrowings from
the pagans; they indicate the external rite wedded to the spirit;
religious acts rising from the heart of man, proceeding in the simple
belief that they are of value before the Face of the Other. In all our
Lord's teachings on the Kingdom, there corresponds to insistence on
act, an interior summoning of the spirit; one must perform one's
religious acts in secret, far from the hope of human reward; one must
bathe the Christian observance in the cleansing spirit of forgiveness.
The insistence is clear that one is not worthy the name Christian
until faith has worked a death to selfishness, inner turmoil, the
will to dominate; the frenetic race for ownership of the universe that
has at root its own penalty, slavery.

The teachings of Matthew's Gospel are basic; they outline the
foundation of the Christian experience; and yet, their very sincerity,
directness, humanity are the guarantee that upon them can be built
the most sublime structures of the Christian spirit. Teresa of Avila,
John of God, Francis Xavier, Charles de Foucauld went to school at
these pages. There is a sort of military masculine directness about
these "Kingdom" chapters; from them, as on a direct line, one is led
to the sublime passages of St. Paul on the elevation of the spirit
by a direct gift of God, to the seventh heaven. It is in this sense that

mysticism has never abandoned the Church, nor the Church the mystic; the preliminary *ascesis* to the life of mysticism is always available to the Church; and even in ages when the great mystic has been conspicuously absent, the Church is still nourished by the doctrine which prepares for the Father's hour the holy few who will bear His gift.

Before the mystical death, an ascetical one is demanded. But in both cases the same principle: that the Father will only take up His abode in the heart that is cleansed and ready. A daily death. The turning out of doors of all selfishness that fills the house with tumult and unrest. The man of the Kingdom moves through life in calm possession of life; he "possesses his soul"; and, possessing himself, he is in radical possession of the universe, since his own soul is the summit and focus of the Divine regard. Out of his life goes the hypocrisy of "charities" performed as legalistic exercises. Out of life goes the charade of prayer that only brings attention from men, and turns away the pure glance of God as from a childish game. And from the purified and lowly heart rises the perfect prayer, taught by the Lord to His Kingdom, and expressing so well inner unity, the will toward peace, holy forgiveness, abandonment to an eternal mercy; all the attitudes of grace that make the Kingdom worthy of its King; the soul, the community, alike blessed by the Divine presence: Jerusalem, city of love.

It is the "Our Father," together with the instructions on trust which follow and amplify the prayer, which forms the truest expression of the spirit of the Kingdom. That spirit is simply the regard of the Son as he faces His loving Father; Thy will be done.

His sons by creation are His sons by grace. They inhabit His Kingdom, not as slaves or even as subjects, but primarily as sons; finally, "I have not called you servants, but friends."

XII

The Saints

In "The Shepherd of Hermas" the writer encounters an old woman whose identity is a mystery to him. " 'Who is this aged woman, from whom you received the little book?' 'The sibyl,' I replied. . . . 'You are wrong, for it is not she. . . .' 'Who is it, then?' 'The Church.' 'Why is she aged?' I then asked. 'Because she was created first, before all else; that is why she is aged. . . . It was for her the world was made.' " Men of faith are obliged, because of their limited stance in time, to view the great Plan of God piecemeal, and even to attribute to the Divine Intelligence a series of decrees, where in fact there was only one inclusive, eternal, total act of love; but faith has to go peering and poking in its own twilight, and the best it can bring forth is a series of accurate but highly inadequate statements; expressing, as best human language can, a love story that included every man born into this world.

On a certain spring afternoon in an obscure Roman province, a despised tributary, occurs the execution of an almost unknown man; and with the finger of God a visible line is traced from that hillside to every man's doorstep. God's intention is older than time, more durable than love, stronger than death. And the years that are a frightful mystery to men are no obstacle to Him; as He sees the world, as He assembles things, as He would explain them, all men are grouped around the cross; all belong there, it was for all and for each; "Christ died for the sake of the Church. . . ."

Or we go back some thousands of years further. "Imagine," St. Augustine says, "a great statue, a colossus, shaken and brought to earth by an upheaval; a statue so noble that its fragments have touched all the world." Original sin literally broke Adam to bits— all his descendants, meant to form with him a living, noble unity, lay in the dust, useless, almost forgotten; until Christ should come, to reassemble the fragments into a more marvelous unity than before. "He gathers all the elect from the four winds, that is to say, from the whole world. . . . Adam is thus scattered through the globe. Set in one place, he fell; and as it were, broken small, he has filled the whole world. But the divine mercy gathered up the fragments from every side, forged them in the fire of love, and welded into one what had been broken."

The image of the statue is little short of inspired, because it illuminates the great work of unity accomplished in Christ. His coming to earth was for the Church: *Christus propter ecclesiam venit.* In the beginning God had marvelously created human nature; sin had all but destroyed the work; it remained for Him now to effect a more marvelous healing; a building up of the new Adam to His image, so that through all time this restored race would show back to the Father the features of the Beloved Son.

And this Church of Christ, how shall one define it, in terms that will not suppress or erase any of its essential qualities; that, in keeping them all firmly in view, will not exaggerate one at the expense of any other? What definition will be more than a figure of speech, and more than a formula, and will approach the mystery without violating it? The difficulties are not inconsiderable. Salvation is in and through the Church, a gift to the individual; yet it touches the whole body of the Church, it is essentially a social gift as well. It is each member that is to be saved, but by union with the Body. Christ died for all men; yet all men are not in fact saved. The Church welcomes as living, operable members every man summoned to her by the Father; she will bless every condition of life, every effort of culture and learning; no one is to be excluded on grounds of human unworthiness; neither the rich, who must become poor men in spirit;

nor the poor, who are promised enrichment in her. Yet, in spite of
ideal formulae, the visible Church after some two millennia on this
earth, remains a minority; and, compared with the growth of the
nations, a shrinking minority in time. And again, to correct a preoccupation with mere statistics, the voice of grace is heard: the
Church in essence will never be a matter of mere numbers; she is a
mystery; a living being, filled with self-knowledge and constancy and
self-diffusion; and the life within her is its own law. So we come
at length to St. Paul's great statement: "You are the Body of Christ,
and member for member." Richest and most exact of all formulae,
because in these few words he implies all her spiritual, living qualities, allows an immense area for contemplation around a familiar figure, and still stops short reverently before the mystery.

It would be interesting to speculate briefly on the reasons that
impelled Paul to deal with the Church under the figure of "body."
Granting always the process of the Holy Spirit in such a choice, it
remains fundamental that his preaching, in order to be effective, had
to reach his people at a point where their meager knowledge was
capable of dealing with the tremendous mystery. And all men, of
course, are most familiar with the fact of a living composite of body
and soul. Very early in his experience of creation, the child discovers himself; and as he advances toward manhood his reflective
powers do not merely touch upon his being at this or that tangent, by
chance; but the body, as possessed, becomes "connatural" to his
consciousness, so that finally a man predicates of himself what he
has absorbed, primarily and continually, from the life of the senses:
I am a living body.

And as maturity advances, so the content of the predication
spreads outward; harmoniously, without effort, as long as the health
of the psychic and affective life is not impaired. In quality, a new
depth of self-knowledge reveals to him the endless possibility of the
human experience; experience which is of irreplaceable importance
to the person, since it conveys, in a thousand delicate ways, the pain
and glory of being human. Acceptance and rejection, sense of community, the ability to love, rejoicing in gifts of emotion and sensibility; through the years, the primitive judgment is infinitely enriched
and expands into a complicated harmonious structure, as the heart

of a crystal grows, or as a first cell, by the dynamism of its form, develops into an organism.

And as with self-knowledge and self-love, so with the social gifts; the knowledge and love of others. In extensive power, the original identification of the self now sends its invisible feelers in the direction of the human family. A "thou" exists, with rights that equal one's own; with a sense of inviolability, with needs that only the "I" can answer. A common source in creation, a common destiny is embraced; the riches of possessing others in a love which deserves the great word "fraternal." An abhorrence of any system of thought, any course of action, which would reduce persons to objects, which would dare to manipulate them at one's own whim, or summon them into one's presence merely to serve a destructive selfishness. Does not an attitude of altruism define the high tides of life upon earth, when men who through no fault of their own lived without the gift of faith still deserve to be called the triumphs of the race—Socrates, Buddha, Virgil?

And in such a way, perhaps, according to St. Paul, man was prepared in its greatest men and women for the Gift that would come to them. Men who refused to allow the ideal of "the body" to die on the earth refused to allow inner and social anarchy to sweep man into a sterile hell, where every other "I" had become a natural enemy, the projection of the enmity within. And by such a natural typology, the body as physical and moral unity, man would be prepared, darkly but truthfully, for the hour of God.

In the good news of Paul, a primitive people had encountered the crisis of salvation. To slaves and the poor, without education or great natural gifts, "not many wise, in the world's fashion, not many powerful, not many well-born"—to these the word had come. "So it was brethren, when I came to you and preached Christ's message to you, I did so without any high pretensions to eloquence or to philosophy." Also, one might add, without any pretense to a highly technical or exact physiology; but armed with the primitive experiences of the body, in growth, action, repose; in its variety and unity, in the interaction and compensation of the members—with all these, the apostle approaches the mystery revealed to men in Christ: "You are one body, with a single spirit; each of you, when he was called,

called in the same hope; with the same God, the same Father of all, Who is above all things, pervades all things, and lives in all of us. . . ."

And over and above the common datum of brotherhood in Christ, the individual persists; he is not extinguished. Indeed, his individuality is preserved and intensified within the Body: "But each of us has received his own special grace, dealt out to him by Christ's gift. . . . Some He has appointed to be apostles, some to be prophets, others to be evangelists, or pastors, or teachers. . . ." Grace does not destroy the individual in ordering him more closely to the Body; it restores his truest identity. Limb or organ apart from the organism no longer deserves, in any true sense, the name "member" at all; it is simply an amputation. By unity within the Body, by fulfilling its vocation to service and usefulness, it discovers itself and is identifiable to others. So with the mystical Reality: the individual grace, the tenacity of self-realization, responsibility and love, all have their place: "These are to order the lives of the faithful . . . to minister to their needs, build up the frame of Christ's Body, until we all realize our common unity through faith in the Son of God, and fuller knowledge of Him."

Now man knows himself intimately and painfully as an individual, but this knowledge receives its Divine corrective in the knowledge and love of the Body, the common cords, not only of Adam but of Christ, Who orders and unites all: "We are to follow the truth in a spirit of charity, and so to grow up, in everything, into a due proportion with Christ Who is our Head."

The following of the truth, however, is not the only function of man at his best. The man with a passion only for knowledge, with a hunger for the truth only as matter of self-interest or speculation, is still far short of the Pauline idea; he is, in fact, really a caricature of man. It is not knowledge only, or even primarily, that perfects the Christian or the Body of Christ; it is charity. Until man loves, he does not know himself, he has no least possibility of reaching what Paul calls "perfect manhood," of swinging wide the mystery of the Church. Only love reveals what the Body is, and what it is doing; because the Church is essentially love in action. So the metaphor of Paul expands—We are the Body of Christ; the Body is destined for growth, for maturity, for manhood; the growth is attained through "following the truth"; but the following is to be done "in a spirit of charity" (Eph. 4:15). It is with the entrance of charity to the discussion that the mind of Paul takes fire. Charity illuminates the mystery of the Church, while protecting it with a Divine delicacy from a presumption that would attempt to force the mystery, and in so doing, destroy all possibility of welcome into its holy arcana.

For the Church has been wedded, body and soul, to Christ. Christ has surrendered His Body to the rigors of sacrificial love, as the good spouse to the beloved. Love has sundered its secrets. Love has proven its name, its nature, its function, has handed over its most precious gifts, to the beloved. This is the capital notion in the whole Pauline complex of the Church; this is the word of immense mystery and immense revelation. Love organizes and unifies the body (Eph. 4:16); it gives each limb the active power it needs; by love, "each limb achieves its natural growth, building itself up." Just as the act of marriage, the act of supreme surrender and mutual trust, is a spiritual symbol of a union of wills, so love is the key to the unity between the Divine Lover and the redeemed Body. By Christ's supreme act of love, His surrender on the cross, His self-consciousness is delivered over to the Church; He whispers his identity to the loved one. To its last fiber the Spouse will now be filled with Him, His designs and dreams, the substantial Mystery of the Father which is manifest in Himself, the truth of the Trinity and grace, the privileges of His mother.

Now the Church can declare to the Word Incarnate, in literal fact: together, we form a single idea of the Creator. In You is all my destiny.

And the love of Christ for the Church, as all true marital love, will be marked by two great realities; fidelity and fruitfulness. When St. Paul is speaking of marriage, he immediately turns to this greater reality of which marital union is the living symbol: "Husbands, love your wives, as Christ loved the Church, and delivered Himself up for her." If the love is a fact, the self-donation is the immediate proof, the evidence. It is an impossibility, derived by the very fidelity of God, that Christ our Lord should turn aside from us, that He should forget the creation that has cost His Blood. "He sits at the right hand of the Father, always interceding for us." The passage of centuries make no difference; the temporal cycles beat in vain against these wounds whose presence in heaven is testimony of a love which refuses to grow weary, to be disillusioned or put off by the continuing affront of sin.

So the act by which our Lord "delivered himself" has not worked a merely speculative good in the Church; certainly it has rendered it knowledgeable of Him; but with an immediate consequence: the transmission of "that mind which is in Christ Jesus" has reproduced in her, not only His divine and human self-consciousness, but the energy to do what He has done; to continue His actions in time. So it is not stating the whole case to say that the Church repeats as her own the Name of Jesus in the world, with a plenitude of authority and an utter assurance; for it was not an abstraction, an idea, a new knowledge, that was born on Calvary; it was the communion of saints. The love of Christ for men is fruitful, it brings to birth all those men and women who in suffering, in combat, in triumph render witness to the double efficiency of the death of Christ; an efficiency of truth, but also an efficiency of love in action. It was the saints, then, as Paul understands them, the members of Christ in combat, who were the firstborn of the dying Christ. In their direction His Blood was poured in greatest abundance.

But the saints were born not as isolated phenomena, but as kneaded and pressed into a common mold and feature; into the communion of saints. And the saint, as a member of the Church, may be defined as the one in whom the double operation of knowledge and love of Jesus Christ has shown most gloriously. It is the saint who knows Christ most accurately; precisely because that knowledge, a gift of grace, has passed over instantaneously to love; knowledge and love have been pressed by the anguish of life into a single living ferment.

The grace of Calvary, then, mediated by the Church in this or that century, lives intact in the saints with a double function: to perpetuate the knowledge and love of Jesus which inundated the Church from the open wound of the Savior. One cannot but be struck by the luminous presence of knowledge and love in the saints, waiting upon their natural gifts, extending their example radiantly through time, cutting them free from the corruption of merely natural effort, keeping their features intact for all generations. With grace enlightening their minds and wills, humanity finds in them a new possibility. It is true that in certain of them, knowledge of sources and development of dogma, of the Divine scheme of things may have been minimal from a scientific point of view; but their love was always divinely excessive; more, their knowledge of the science of life, its inner meaning, has accuracy, an intensity, an inner serenity that mark it as the product of grace. Because they know human life, they go without danger into any area of life; in the Church the paradoxes of grace are a commonplace: the unlettered saint confounding the doctors; the learned doctor upon the scaffold; the man or woman of extraordinary social talent finding fulfillment in contemplative obscurity; the contemplative leading a crusade, the child confounding the tyrant, the old man singing a song in the fire of martyrdom, the mystic sitting down with princes; the prince in the hairshirt, the hermit returning to set the Kingdom aright. In all of them a Divine principle has come to flower; an inner logic is directing things to a Divine outcome; in all of them, the Church, mediating Jesus in time, is still bringing forth, with a truly Divine fecundity, the sons and daughters who bear Christ into the world.

A further precision. The Church is to guard scientifically the name and nature of God throughout time. She alone is guaranteed an exact tradition in regard to His identity and His works. This custody of truth is free from all corruption and vicissitude; outside her it simply does not exist; she is alone the child of promise. And the promise is given her as to a living body; every revealed truth is seminally present in her consciousness from the beginning, to be elaborated and revealed progressively, following the laws of growth. She is a law unto herself, deciding when the time is opportune for making explicit this or that truth. Now history shows that the action whereby she hands over the fruits of her contemplation to men has followed a certain rhythm in time. At some periods her self-revelation was marked by great brilliance and profundity; at others, this accidental advance is scarcely noticeable at all. Wars or persecution or inner trials slow the process; at such periods the Church is content to ponder in her heart those things which were her possession in implicit fullness from apostolic times.

One can speak, then, of periods that were comparatively barren in doctors of the Church, in encyclicals or theological definitions. But at these times there has been another mark to her credit; another sign that her presence in the world is literally Divine; and those springs have never dried, and never will. It is the presence of saints in her midst, saints who by a witnessing other than scientific bore her features, did her work among men, were nourished at her sacraments, testified to her Divine birth. And it is precisely this witness of the saints that will never be wanting in the Church: they testify to the presence of One among men Who can clearly be discerned across their lives and deaths; and this presence, multiplied in secret, in public, in high places and unlikely, in answers before judges and the more painful encounter with one's own conscience, this presence lives on and can be discerned, if one will attend. "I am with you all days, even to the consummation of the world." Lost in the Church, they testify to the fullness of Jesus within her. Acting through the Church, they start the rhythms of example and prayer that nourish others yet unborn. Being closest to the Church by grace, they are the most accurate and trustworthy witness to her expanding self-knowledge. Most honorable of her members, they render her incarnate and glorious, extending her action, bearing her presence into the visible and invisible world. Through them "I am with you all days, even to the consummation of the world."

XIII

Until He Come

A fruitful point of departure for a study of the relation of the Church to history might be summed up in the formula: The Church and history interpenetrate; but neither gives over its identity to the other. History is in the Church, and the Church is in history. Perhaps a more dynamic form could be given this principle; it would also be true to say: The Church makes history, and history makes the Church.

The Church makes history quite literally because history would not bear the same character today, would not have taken the same course in the past, had not her action taken place on it. Even during periods when Christianity as an external influence does not seriously deflect the course of things, it still is true to say that the mark of her moral judgment rests on the world; that the world must take her conscience into consideration; that whatever respect for the moral law, whatever residual idea of God remains in it, it owes to her. She makes history more and more "transformable" to herself, looking with hope to a future when the world can be completely leavened; but in the meantime she is watchful and active lest paganism completely claim the world for its own Kingdom. She continues to impose on the world her respect for natural virtue, which her revelation has so clarified and strengthened; the redemptive value of time, its serious reality as a stage of action; the meaning of freedom, without which history is an eviscerated series of events moving in chains —by teaching these she in fact preserves in time the very ingredients of a genuine history.

In a less formal sense, the Church makes history because her rites, her sacrifice, her organization move visibly through time, and at every stage of time are so manifest that they cannot be ignored by men of good will; they demand from history a value-judgment on what they represent; indefectibility, Catholicity, holiness, unity.

History also makes the Church. Though her essence escapes it, world history still affects her painfully and deeply, because her Master has committed her to the world. So it is quite accurate to say that forms of government favor or deter her progress, that heresy harms her grievously; that a certain mission, project, form of the apostolate, would have flourished but for human blindness. While she lives in history, the Church will never free herself from the vicissitudes of history; the catastrophes of nature, ignorance, human limitation, sin in her midst. Nor will she cease to be glorified and aided by the natural values of the world, as men have brought them to flower in a certain period. Her features are more glorious because forms of art, national literatures, medical discoveries, justice under law reveal themselves as true to man and infused with natural genius. All these things say what she says. In being true to the human, men are not denying or diminishing her.

What then of sacred history during the period of time until the second coming of the Lord? The fruits of the Spirit will be active, rendering the Church progressively leaven, light, salt of the earth. The Spirit will be working toward universal unity and interior peace; a unity transcending nation and time, and binding the Church in heaven and on earth in an organic, diversified, active Body of love. In the vision of heaven will reside the hope of the Church militant; it will at the same time act as a stimulus to action, a nostalgic taste of home.

Power: a supernatural one. She is the Body of Christ; she has power over the Body of Christ; she receives It for her joy and upbuilding; It is the source of all her aspiration and desire. With the death of the Risen Christ renewed on her altars and in the bodies of her sons, she goes forward, assured of the favor of the Father, to make those permanent and burning impressions on the shifty matter of time. Because His Body and Spirit are working in her, she is able to turn progressively His features of compassion and assurance on the world; the same tenderness and authority with which He had faced His people. As He knew Who He was, she knows her identity; and in the impetus of that assurance she takes time, civilizations, cultures, scientific discovery, all things human to herself, without being essentially committed or even accidentally corrupted by them.

Until He come: a phrase gathering into three words all her faith in His promise; He will return to rescue, witness, bind, perfect, and reward; all her hopes are summed up in her desire to see His Divine Humanity again, turned to the Church as to a mirror reflecting His own face; all her love awaits Him—since she knows He comes to judge her works against His own, and expects to find in her the same wounds which love inflicted upon Him.

In the meantime, what does time mean to her? It means everything, and it means nothing.

It means everything because she is conscious of His return at any moment, and is conscious that the world still awaits redemption through her faith and works. Time means everything to her, because it is given her to trade, until the return of the Merchant, demanding to what uses she put her talents. In the meantime, where her direct action on men is impossible, she is to move among them with prudence and hope, not pressing her claims beyond measure, but always showing the charity rooted in the Body, a concern for temporal welfare, sympathy and welcome for the genius of man, raising her voice whenever justice is endangered, waiting for the hour when the blind will be stirred by her Spirit to know her for who she is.

While she awaits the Master, then, she is no loiterer in the marketplace. Her own complex, malleable, and tireless charity defines the greatness of her labors. To the Father she shows the true image of His Son in sacrifice and prayer; to the poor, a mother in truth; to the persecutor, a victim for Jesus; to the liberal secularist, a mystery or an abomination—but a reality as alive to the value of the world, of time, of justice and peace, as himself; to the other religions, an unswerving constancy, holding to her irrefragable claim of truth while fully sympathetic to their sincerity of heart; summoning to her presence whatever is true, whatever noble, whatever good; turning her face, as did her Lord, only from that unbearable sin which is against His Spirit.

But time also means nothing to her. Is she still in infancy on the earth, or will the Bridegroom return to her today? It makes no difference; she is ready. Her treasure is totally uncovered from the field where it lay; her leaven active in the Mass, her pearl of great price in her hand. She holds up her good works, she is heavy with her fruit, she is that tree whose seed was no more than a dust, but to which the birds come from the corners of the earth; for horizon, direction, refreshment, shelter, rest.

Since the sacrifice of Christ is renewed in and through her, she is assured at every moment of the welcome of the Father. By the works of the Spirit in her, her children move forward to glory, refreshed and strengthened by the sacraments she has administered to them: sonship, strength, forgiveness, grace of state.

The moral teaching of Christ was addressed primarily to her with the promise that "if anyone love me, he will keep my word, and my Father will love him." So she continues to fulfill the beatitudes in the world, filling the lowly ones of the nations with the fire of Pentecost; the poor of spirit, the meek, the mourners, the merciful, the clean of heart, the peacemakers; she has brought them to birth in her own Body; consequently, she knows them and they know her.

Her love is already perfect at every moment, because of the Son Who died for her and the Spirit Who lives in her. She has followed to the letter the charity preached by her Master; she loves her enemies, she does good to them that hate her, she prays for those who calumniate and revile her. And because of her perfect love, she stands as the literal fulfillment of the astounding counsel of Christ: "Be ye perfect as your heavenly Father is perfect."

The Spirit that informs her is eternal, and renders her immortal; but since she is placed in the world to save it, she is truly affected by the fair and foul of human weather. Eternal and living in time: in this paradox is revealed the sublimity and height of the synthesis she has achieved in Christ Jesus. Since she is eternal, she is tranquilly at work in time. Since eternity is promised her, and its seed is already within her, she has time for everyone and everything. Since by the grace she is already at rest in the Trinity, she can take the most audacious risks in time.

In regard to the members of Christ's Body, sure of the power of grace in their souls, she puts them in her service, to the most diverse and rigorous works under the sun; some to race against time with a Divine impatience for souls; others buried in time as in a grave, in time as a reflection of eternity. Contemplatives and apostles, they are animated by her one Spirit, busy at her one task, visibly and invisibly affecting the same souls.

In her own depths, she is conscious of the eternal as of her own soul. And being totally immersed in the Holy Spirit, she echoes in holy activity the question of the Master, "Is not the soul more than the body?" Not to say that the body is valueless; but to compare it to the soul is to illuminate the value of each. So the Church can show endless solicitude toward the despised and abandoned; and on the other hand, can send her greatest men and women into circumstances where early martyrdom will be a high probability. She is spendthrift with time and its works, and a most rigorous miser with whatever concerns eternity, in the sense that she will immolate the energies and lives of her apostles with prodigality, in order to save men or guarantee the conditions of salvation.

Time is everything to her; on its revolving stage, in its expanding world, she releases the works and prayer of her ministers and her baptized. Time is to her a perpetual springtime, with unlimited opportunity for the planting; time is a perpetual autumn, with labors and harvest to try her energies to the utmost.

So, while her essence escapes history, and lives already before the Trinity, she is still a visible sign among the nations, evolving with them and they in her, affecting history profoundly by her passing, affected by history in a thousand conditions of growth and prosperity, reverse and persecution, honor and dishonor; Until He Come.